Ireland's loyalty to the mass

Ireland's loyalty to the Mass

by

FR. AUGUSTINE HAYDEN, O.F.M. CAP.

SOPHIA INSTITUTE PRESS
Manchester, New Hampshire

Originally published in 1933 by Sands & Company in London.
Printed in the United States of America. All rights reserved.

Cover by Joshua Facemyer, Impressus Art LLC (ImpressusArt.com)

Cover image: *Aloysius O'Kelly* (1854–1936),
Mass in a Connemara Cabin, 1883 (public domain)

Imprimi Potest:
Fr. Colmanus, O.M.Cap.
Vic. Prov. Hib.
August 28, 1933

Nihil Obstat:
Joannes Gray,
Censor librorem.

Imprimatur:
✠ Andreas Joseph, O.S.B.
Archiep. S. Andr. et Ed.
Edimburgi
Die ult October 1933

Scripture quotations are taken from the Douay-Rheims edition of the Old and New Testaments.

Sophia Institute Press
Box 5284, Manchester, NH 03108
1-800-888-9344
www.SophiaInstitute.com

Sophia Institute Press is a registered trademark of Sophia Institute.

paperback ISBN 978-1-64413-908-0

ebook ISBN 978-1-64413-909-7

Library of Congress Control Number: 2023939932

To the Irish everywhere who love the Mass
this little book is dedicated

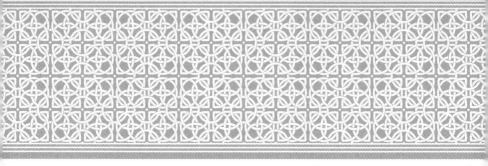

"*The Mass* is superior even to the abiding presence of our Blessed Lord in the Most Holy Sacrament....

"*The Mass* is the very means He has given us to enable us to join with Him, and to share with Him in the sacrifice of the *Cross*.

"*The Mass* ... is the very life of the Church, the secret of her holiness and vitality. No wonder that the spirits of darkness should have inspired the heretic with hatred for the Mass, for they know that when they strike at the Mass, they strike at the heart of the Church."

Most Rev. Dr. Sheehan
Sydney

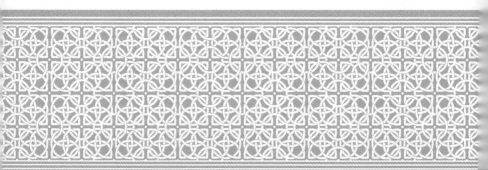

contents

ireland's loyalty to the mass

england's breach with rome

From the golden hour in which St. Patrick as bishop said his first Mass on Irish soil down to the coming of the Normans, love of the Blessed Eucharist was one of the dominant characteristics of the Irish race. The advent of the foreigner, it is true, inaugurated a great conflict, but this was concerned with territory and not with religion. Both the invaders and the natives were Catholics, and while the latter fought to hold what the former sought to seize, churches and chapels, monasteries and shrines began to spring up in great profusion throughout the country, testifying to the fragrant fact that from the simple faith of the Norman flowed a still richer manifestation of devotion toward our eucharistic Lord and King.

It was not till the third decade of the sixteenth century that the conflict assumed a religious aspect. On the causes of this change, there are differences of opinion, just as there are differences of opinion regarding the mind of the young century itself in which it occurred. But if we would have a clear and distinct idea of the religious struggle in Ireland, we must first consider briefly the genesis and evolution of England's breach with Rome.

When Henry VIII succeeded to the throne of his father in 1509, England was a completely Catholic country, and nothing seemed more unlikely than that during his reign it should renounce its allegiance to the See of Rome. Between that country and the Holy See there had been, it is true, from time to time some difficulties and misunderstandings, but these were chiefly in the temporal domain, and in spite of them, Englishmen had always treated the Holy Father with great respect as their spiritual head. With the revolt of Luther and the subsequent chaotic speculation and wild denunciation that spread over Northern Germany, the young king had no sympathy whatever. Every honest historian admits that he was a devoted son of the Catholic Church till the pert and ill-fated Anne Boleyn crossed his path.

Of this, abundant proof is furnished by two events that occurred in 1521. On the twelfth of May, in St. Paul's Churchyard, near the famous St. Paul's Cross, the papal brief against Luther was solemnly published in the presence of a great multitude, and all his writings burned. In addition to this, on the fourteenth of September, the English envoy, Dr. Clerk, presented to the pope a splendidly bound copy of a book that the king himself had substantially written. The book was entitled "A Defense of the Seven Sacraments against Luther," and bore the dedication: "England's King sends Leo X this work as a sign of faith and friendship." The Holy Father was overjoyed and, in deference to the wishes of many, conferred on the king the noble title of "Defender of the Faith." It is interesting to note, and not without a touch of humor, that this title still remains on the coinage and arms of English sovereigns, while the royal polemic against the apostate monk is now exhibited in the Vatican Library side by side with the love letters of its author to Anne Boleyn.[1]

This young lady of the court was, undoubtedly, the evil genius of Henry's life, and less than six years after the presentation of the "Defense," men were speaking of the strong fascination that she was already exercising over him. This fascination soon increased, and

[1]   Pastor, *The History of the Popes*, vol. 8, pp. 442–43.

before long, she alone held sway over the mind and heart and conduct of the captive king.

Henry's conscience became strangely troubled, and after eighteen years of happy wedded life, he began, in the April of 1527, to express scruples regarding the validity of his marriage with Catherine of Aragon, who had failed to give him a male heir. He applied to the pope for an annulment of the marriage and, because Clement VII did not grant his petition, threatened to repudiate the authority that he had already acknowledged by his appeal. His love for the papacy began to cool, then Anne becoming more resolute, Henry found himself committed to action where he had at first only intended to threaten.

The court, legitimately set up in London to try the case of Catherine, was adjourned, and for having consented to the adjournment, Cardinal Wolsey was publicly insulted and later summarily dismissed. After this no one dared to interfere, and events marched quickly to a disastrous conclusion. Henry was inexcusably weak before a woman's determined insistence, Catherine was banished from the court, Anne was installed in her place, and to save the coming child's succession, Henry married her secretly on the twenty-fifth of January 1533.

For his skillful managing of this delicate matter, Thomas Cromwell, already the trusted adviser of the king, was rewarded by being raised to the dignity of chancellor for life. In 1534, the Act of Supremacy was passed, and the ancient dependence on Rome being terminated, Henry was declared "the only supreme head on earth of the Church of England." Cromwell, though only a layman, was made vicar-general and had now a free hand in carrying out his policy of the suppression of the monasteries, which would not only abolish monasticism in England but replenish the empty coffers of more than the king.

It was to Cromwell that Henry, having squandered his great wealth, first applied to find a way out of his monetary embarrassment, and from some suggestion of his sprang "the concerted attack upon the Church." After having given expression to this opinion,

J. S. Fletcher[2] goes on to say very deliberately: "I believe he turned to Cromwell, a smart and crafty business man, for financial advice; I believe that Cromwell coolly pointed to the Church." The complaints made against the monasteries did not come from the people, who attested their loyalty to them in risings that only narrowly escaped success. "The voices raised against the monks were those of Cromwell's agents, of the cliques of the new men and of his hireling scribes who formed a crew of as truculent and as filthy libelers as ever disgraced a revolutionary cause. The later centuries have taken their tale in good faith, but time is showing that the monasteries, up to the day of their fall, had forfeited neither the goodwill, the veneration, nor the affection of the English people."[3]

The suppression of these hospitable institutions went on simultaneously with the preaching of the royal supremacy, and papal dues as well as monastic wealth were being gathered and kept in England. Into the exchequer of Henry they were indeed supposed to flow, but there were certain families who saw very clearly that they could divert a great deal of this money into their own pockets. When these two sources of revenue were combined, "it became of desperate importance to this new, rapacious, unscrupulous, irreligious class that the old order should not be restored." In promoting the suppression and the supremacy, Browne, the English apostate monk, was most zealous. Ever alert, he soon became known as Cromwell's "right-hand man in all things unlawful" and "the unscrupulous agent he employed in furtherance of all his schemes." He served well the man who was nearest to the throne and must now be rewarded for his accommodating servility and unholy activity.

The archbishopric of Dublin had been vacant for nineteen months. Browne, being chosen by the king for the position, was

[2]   Fletcher, *The Reformation in Northern England*, p. 22.
[3]   Gasquet, *Henry the Eighth and the English Monasteries*, p. xx.

consecrated without any reference to the pope at Lambeth on Sunday the nineteenth of March 1536. In the following July, he arrived in Dublin, six or seven weeks after an Irish Parliament, not without great opposition, had passed the Act of Supremacy declaring "the King our Sovereign Lord, the only supreme head on earth of the whole Church of Ireland." Anyone refusing to acknowledge him in that capacity, by the taking of an oath if required, exposed himself to danger. He might be punished even with death, as in England, if the refusal were obstinate and repeated, and the same penalty awaited all those who persistently preached against the royal supremacy.

To the advancement of this cause, the king's archbishop now devoted all his efforts, but he did not find it such an easy task. There was discontent and opposition on every side; the king was not pleased with the slow progress of things spiritual, and on the thirty-first of July 1537, he wrote to Edward Staples, bishop of Meath, and also to Browne, charging both with want of devotion in instructing the people and furthering the interests of the king. Browne's reply reveals his real character and is a most pitiful manifestation of the slave-soul of the man. As a fitting climax to his abject protestations, he prays that should he fail in preaching "the gospel of Christ" or "rebuking the papistical power, ... the ground might open and swallow him."

He renewed his efforts, but all in vain. Writing to his friend Cromwell on the eighth of January 1538, he confesses that since his coming he could not "persuade or induce any, either religious or secular, to preach the word of God, or the just title of our most illustrious prince." "The word of God" and "the gospel of Christ" were favorite expressions on the lips of the *reformers*, yet by these they meant not the orthodox teaching of the Catholic Church but the travesty of that teaching that they wished to preach to the people. Not only was the supremacy not preached but eloquent silence reigned in the churches wherever English rule prevailed. Yet, far from the watchful spies and interested officials, in quiet places, the priests exhorted the people to continue in their loyalty to the Holy Father and to hold fast to every tenet of their Faith.

Browne next published a pastoral in which he nibbled at the Catholic doctrines of Confession and Purgatory. The people cared as little for his pastoral as for his preaching, but his indiscreet desire to push the "reform" led to a rupture between himself and the bishop of Meath. "The common voice goeth," complainingly wrote the latter, "that he doth abhor the Mass." To this voice strength was added, and also the appearance of truth, by a phrase that Browne himself used five months later. On the sixth of November, writing to Cromwell, he attacks the Observant Franciscans, whom he had already denounced as the "worst of all others" in their contumacy. He now complains that they had no respect for his authority and ridicules them for their celebration of the "feigned holy Mass."

Cromwell and Cranmer had been for the past few years, and were, at this very time, intriguing with German Lutherans on doctrinal matters, which included the Blessed Eucharist. They both hated the Mass, but for different reasons. Browne knew of their hatred and their intrigues, and though Henry did not, he too felt at last that, even among his own chosen servants, the New Learning was making headway, and that there was something of religious revolution in the air. He resolved, therefore, to enforce the orthodox views that he and the English people held, and that he was determined should be maintained as long as he sat upon the throne.

On the twenty-fourth of June 1539, accordingly, the Six Articles' Statute received the royal assent and became law on the twelfth of July. This statute affirmed Catholic doctrine, especially regarding matters that the innovators wished to change, and commanded that auricular Confession as well as private Masses should be continued in the King's English Church. The doctrines of the Catholic Church Henry upheld consistently. He would have no toleration of Protestantism, and as a proof of his strict impartiality, he sent with equal readiness to the stake or the scaffold Protestants who denied Catholic teaching, especially transubstantiation, and Catholics who refused to acknowledge the ecclesiastical supremacy that he claimed for himself.

In this year also the suppression of the religious houses became general in Ireland, and with the monasteries went also the schools for the education of priests. Few schools of any kind could, in fact, henceforward exist without grave risk, except in the purely Celtic parts, and aspirants to the priesthood had to get away by stealth in merchant vessels bound for Flanders, France, and Portugal. The wealth of jewels, ornaments, and plate belonging to the monastic chapels, Henry ordered to be paid into his own private account, and the lands that were leased out to the Anglo-Normans, he hoped to make a nucleus for the extension of his power in Ireland. The dissolution of the monasteries was often accompanied by bloodshed, and rather than submit to the doctrine of the king's supremacy, many religious suffered imprisonment and death.

The plunder of ecclesiastical possessions in Ireland continued for many years, and so did the official fitful preaching of the supremacy of the king. Henry could indeed suppress the monasteries and convents, but he could not impress the priests nor the people. Not even under the shadow of Dublin Castle could respect be inspired for the royal supremacy, nor adhesion won to what the Four Masters describe as a "heresy and new error," the fruit of "pride, vainglory, avarice, and lust." Not all the terrors of the law, nor the threats of officials, nor the preaching of Browne and Staples could induce the people to surrender. These paid servants of a State Church sometimes quarreled with each other, and being unable to speak a word of Irish, could not make themselves understood by the people. The people, moreover, did not wish to hear them, and nothing that they and others said or did was ever able to effect in Ireland even the shadow of a breach with Rome.

"On the side of Rome," says Fr. Myles Ronan,[4] "was ranged popular feeling, religious tradition, the faith handed down to them through generations, and these had the support of crowds of devoted men who could exhort the people in their own tongue, and whose example was sometimes more eloquent than their words.... In England, Anglicanism was the outcome of national independence; in Ireland, it was the badge of conquest," which interested men were trying to force upon the soul of a people intensely loyal to the Chair of Peter.

In justice, however, to the memory of Henry, we must say that it is now generally admitted he did not intend to make permanent his breach with Rome. "There was no reason why that breach should not have been healed after the deaths of Catherine and Anne Boleyn, had it not been for the opposition of those that had profited financially from the change." It is important that we should remember this, and there is also another matter that we must not overlook.

Though despicably tricked regarding a few things, though hopelessly blinded by flattery and vanity, even to the extent of calling himself the "Vicar of Christ," the king was neither tricked nor blinded so far as to lay even one finger on what had been the center of religious and social life in England and Ireland since the coming of Augustine and Patrick. In both countries, monasteries and convents had been suppressed without justice; shrines and images had been despoiled without shame; episcopal sees had been robbed; chalices had been sold, and even moneys left for Masses for the dead had been filched. But Henry kept hands off one most sacred thing: the Mass itself had been untouched.

No one dared to suggest change in this, because all knew his orthodoxy regarding the Mass. Amid all his moods and whims of temper, in spite of colossal vanity and selfishness, notwithstanding

---

[4] Ronan, *The Reformation in Dublin*, p. 294.

irritability and impetuosity, he remained steadfast to this great "Mystery of Faith." Not only after his pretended scruples about Catherine, not only till his final break with the pope, but to the end, he continued true. Though those who were nearest the throne, such as Cromwell and Cranmer, had plotted against it for years, they dared not utter the faintest whisper of their doings to the king. The destruction of the Holy Sacrifice was the main object of the anti-Catholic Reformation, but Henry stood to the last hour of his life for the Mass.

Even after death, the voice of this wayward and unlovable man spoke loudly in favor of the loveliest, and most festal, and most joyous action on earth. When his will was opened, many things were read therein, but none so touching as the words that sound now so strange and sad. Sadder and stranger they seem in the light of the strong hatred that burned in the heart of the man who knelt by him at the last, and still more in the light of the fierce opposition that soon was to be manifested against what he so earnestly requested should be done, as soon as he was gone. The request is so little known that the words must be quoted here as a fit conclusion to this chapter.

"We do earnestly require and desire the Blessed Virgin, God's Mother, with all the company of heaven, to pray for us … and that there be provided, ordained and set a convenient altar honourably prepared and apparelled, with all manner of things necessary for daily Mass (for my soul), there to be said perpetually while the world shall endure."

CHAPTER 2

The undermining of the mass

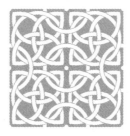

Henry died at Whitehall in the dead of night, on the twenty-sixth of January 1547, while Cranmer held his hand and whispered in his ear. He was succeeded by his only son under the title of Edward VI, who, being but ten years of age, was a king merely in name. The real power lay in the hands of a council of regency nominated in the will of the dead monarch to govern during the minority of his little son. The majority of these men, and the very strongest among them, were "reformers" who were determined to force upon the still Catholic people of England, and to introduce into Ireland, changes in Catholic doctrine and worship that were never contemplated by Henry.

The motive power behind the council, which consisted of sixteen persons, was the necessity of making their position absolutely secure so that no future reaction could imperil the loot they had acquired by the suppression of the monasteries and hospitals and the seizure of parish endowments and guilds. To achieve this security, these men clearly saw that the old Faith, which had given birth to these things, should be abolished. The sacramental idea, with its consecrated priesthood and its sacred property, should be destroyed, and in its stead should be enthroned that more accommodating form of worship called Protestantism, which they had secretly cherished for several years. The central point of this policy and the main object of their attack was the Mass.

The destruction of the Mass, however, was a dangerous enterprise, and cautious procedure was absolutely necessary. Throughout the whole of 1547, accordingly, the old religion was carried on with its accustomed splendor, as if no change were being planned. But in 1548, the secret plans were far advanced, and the first wary move was made toward the general undermining of the Mass.

Mass was associated in the common mind with the Latin language, which represented not only a mysterious sanctity but also a certain universality. So, for those who were bent on the change in religion, the use of the vernacular was essential. It would help to destroy the sense of mystery and, in consequence, limit the power of the clergy. It would advance nationalism, break down the general unity in worship, impair the sacred authority of the universal Church, from priest to pope, and ensure, what the innovators most desired, the destruction of the Adorable Sacrifice.

The new vernacular service was ready at last, and having passed Parliament in January as the first Prayer Book of Edward VI, or the Prayer Book of 1549, it was to come into force on the ninth of the following June. That day at length arrived, and the attempt to foist on the people this service, from which any reference to the sacrificial quality of the Mass had been carefully expunged, was met by a resistance the strength of which could scarcely have been expected. The congregations rose everywhere in splendid revolt. They fought courageously, but having neither military leaders nor effective arms, they were mowed down by well-trained foreign mercenaries, German and Italian, who happened to be then present on English soil.

The heroic protest failed, and the council won. The newly established religion was safe for the time, but Somerset was deprived of the Protectorate, and into his place stepped Warwick, who assumed the title of Northumberland. Parliament met that autumn, and several repressive measures were passed. During the next two years, a vigorous propaganda was carried on, in which foreign preachers and writers aided with voice and pen, as foreign mercenaries had helped with sword and gun. Then the second Prayer Book appeared, which differed little from that now in use in the Church of England, and which was absolutely devoid of every idea of the Real Presence and every suggestion of the Mass.

Meanwhile, the Catholic bishops were being deposed and imprisoned; pictures and images were being removed from the churches; and the work of destruction so thoroughly accomplished that, before long, though bells and organs were spared, there were neither pictures nor altars left. "So long as there is an altar," the venomous Hooper used to say, "the ignorant people will always dream of a sacrifice." The people lost all respect for the desecrated churches and turned them "into common inns or rather into dens and sinks of iniquity." So ran a royal decree published in 1552, the same year in which the second and final Prayer Book was linked with a new Act of Uniformity and ordered to come into force on All Saints' Day.

The innovations attempted in England found no genuine supporter in Ireland, where the challenge to the people's Faith provoked a magnificent loyalty. Even many of those who had accepted the royal supremacy, whether knowing its real import or not, now resolutely refused to go farther. The priests continued to say Mass and the people to assist at it as before. Browne, however, complained that the deputy, Sentleger, was too partial to the papists. Having, therefore, been recalled in April, 1548, he was succeeded by Bellingham, who belonged to the same religious party as Somerset. Arrived in Dublin some weeks later, the new deputy's influence was soon felt, and not long after appeared evidences of desire to pave the way for the changes that he knew were coming. Preaching in his presence, and in that of the council, a certain Scot, probably Mr. Water, condemned, first at Kilmainham, and then during August in Christ

Church, Dublin, "the Mass and other ceremonies." These were the first denunciations of the Holy Sacrifice from an Irish pulpit, but there soon followed another in the same year, and in the same city.

Staples had preached in Dublin on the merely "spiritual" presence of Our Lord in the great Sacrament and against the Catholic doctrine of the Mass. The news of the false teaching spread quickly and, as a letter[5] he wrote to Bellingham's secretary abundantly testifies, provoked the righteous indignation of the people of his own diocese of Meath. "Ye have not heard such rumours," he writes, "as is here all the country over against me." Then he proceeds to mention his grievances, only some of which need be stated here. He was accused of having denied the Sacrament of the Altar, people refused to listen to his sermons, some said he was a heretic, and "one of our lawyers declared to a multitude that it was a great pity that I was not burned for I preached heresy so was I worthy therfor."

But the apex of injury was reached when a beneficed man, whom he himself had promoted, came and, unburdening his soul in great distress, told the bishop how the people were feeling and what they were saying. On inquiring the cause of their changed attitude, the bishop was promptly assured it was because he had "taken open part with the State, that false heretic, and preached against the Sacrament of the Altar." The clergyman concluded by saying his lordship had more curses heaped on him than there were hairs on his head, that the country was ready to eat him, that he feared more than he dared say, and besought him "for Christ's sake" not to go to Navan where he had heard he intended preaching. Staples concludes his letter by asking the secretary's advice, saying, "As God shall judge me I am afraid of my life divers ways."

There was evidently a speeding-up of the work of "reform" with the coming of Sir Edward Bellingham, who is described as "a zealous

---

[5]   Shirley, *Original Letters*, no. 7.

Protestant and a brave soldier." He was aware that Sentleger had been recalled because of his lukewarmness regarding the "Reformation." He knew how the attack against the Mass was being maneuvered in England, but he did not know Ireland so well as his predecessor, and neither in political nor in religious things was his discretion equal to his bravery. During his deputyship, says Hollis,[6] the first attempts were made to introduce Protestantism, which came hand-in-hand with a policy of aggression. Bellingham attempted to extend the area of English influence, and castles were established both at Athlone, in order to dominate Connacht, and at Leighlin Bridge, to dominate Munster.

This stupid and fanatical soldier was playing a more important part in history than he guessed, and according to the writer just now quoted, it was Bellingham who raised in Ireland an issue more fundamental than that of race or family — the issue of religion. He raised it in such a way that from his day to ours the Irish question has been predominantly a religious question. His policy soon produced mischief in every quarter; insurrection followed insurrection, and though all were savagely suppressed, it was quite evident that both money and blood were poured out in vain. In 1549, Irish poems were forbidden, "except to the King," and later, harps were broken wherever found. Yet there was but little advancement of English power, and none at all of the reformed doctrines. The council in Ireland were constantly complaining of the lord deputy's doings, with the result that he was recalled in this year, and Sentleger returned once more.

Finding Irish affairs in such a dangerous position and knowing the temper of the people, he was anxious to resume his former conciliatory measures in religious as in civil matters. Browne, now following very closely the progress of things in England, strongly disapproved of this policy. But to all the remonstrances of the archbishop, the deputy would reply, "Your matter of religion will mar all."

---

6   Hollis, *The Monstrous Regiment*, p. 180.

In February 1551, however, he received orders to introduce into Ireland the new liturgy, which "we ... have ... caused ... to be translated into our mother-tongue of this realm of England," and to have it used in all churches.

With these orders of the English Privy Council began in our midst the infamous attack on the holiest Sacrament of our Faith. The saying of Mass was made a penal offense. Sentleger had no sympathy with this aggressive move, but he deemed it safer to obey his English masters, though he knew well that no one in Ireland, with the exception of a few officials, wanted the first Book of Common Prayer.

Accordingly, he assembled the bishops on the first of March 1551, and attempted to force its adoption on them. Bravely led by Dowdall, the primate, the Irish bishops presented a bold front. Neither the king's commands nor his deputy's suavities could subdue or deceive them. "Then shall every illiterate fellow read Mass," said Dowdall, and after a heated discussion, he left the assembly in great wrath, followed by several other prelates. Browne, of course, with his usual servility, was ready to receive orders of "Our Gracious King," but the only ones to follow his example were Staples of Meath, Lancaster of Kildare, and Travers of Leighlin.

In the teeth of such determined opposition, it was obviously impossible to force the acceptance of the Book of Common Prayer. Almost everywhere, Mass was celebrated as before, and the people assisted at it as usual. The offenders were too numerous to punish, and the deputy was unwilling to enforce the law. He went so far as to say it would have been better to avoid all this "hurly-burly" by letting the religious question alone. This so annoyed the English ministers that, in May, they recalled him and sent Sir James Crofts as his successor.

Crofts convened another meeting of the bishops in 1552. As with the one in the preceding year, it was held in Dublin, but proved as great a failure. Though appointed by the king and consecrated without the authority of the pope, Dowdall, a thorough Englishman of good character, in conduct and purpose the very antithesis of Browne, once more stood firm as a rock. Now rejecting the spiritual supremacy of the king, and supporting the supreme authority of the pope, he repudiated all efforts to introduce the new liturgy and to destroy the ancient Mass. Deprived of the honors of the primacy that were given to Browne, and fearing measures that might involve his life, he left the country but came back in triumph in the reign of Mary.

On the second of February 1553, Bale was consecrated bishop of Ossory, according to the new form for the purpose, attached to the second Book of Common Prayer. This book had not so far been sanctioned by an Irish Parliament, and hence its adoption on this occasion, instead of the Roman Pontifical, was not "without opposition from the popishly-inclined clergy." In spite of all, however, this king's bishop had his way in Christ Church, Dublin, but when, very soon after, he tried to impose his will on the priests and people of his own diocese, he found the opposition of a somewhat sharper kind.

Bale was the bitterest and most violent of all the reformers, but his first public proclamation of Edward's "reform" and denunciation of the "Popish Mass," in the city of Kilkenny, provoked an outburst of loyalty that he never forgot. The faithful were furious and could not restrain themselves. A great tumult arose, and five of his own attendants were slain before his eyes. He himself was forced to fly from the fury of the populace and shut himself up behind the iron gates of his castle. There he had to remain until the arrival of the civil magistrate at the head of five hundred soldiers.

A little over five months later, Edward was no more. During his reign of six years, little had been accomplished in Ireland in the way of "reform" of the Mass. Cautiously as the innovators proceeded in England, they proceeded still more cautiously in Ireland. The English government had indeed done its best in a slow and subtle manner, but the Irish people proved too strong in the Faith and too loyal to the Mass.

The liturgy in English had, it is true, been introduced into the country; a move had even been made to translate it into Irish so as to capture popular sympathy; and the second Prayer Book had also found its way into the Pale.[7] But even within this restricted area, its influence was very slight, and Protestant historians honestly admit that the "reform" was a distinct failure. When the news of the death of Edward reached Ireland, the people breathed freely once more, for they knew that Mary would be his successor and that she was a fervent Catholic. Hope was visible everywhere, and the joy that we know filled the hearts of the people in one particular city may be taken as a sure index of their feelings throughout the rest of the country.

The news did not reach Kilkenny till more than a fortnight later, and Bale, who had not yet been six months in office, has left us an account of how it was received in the city by the Nore on the twenty-fifth of July. From this rather scurrilous document,[8] it will be sufficient to extract some passages that bear upon our subject. "The priests," he says, "were as pleasantly disposed as might be," and he hastens to admit that the reason was "King Edward was dead, and that they were in hope to have up their masking masses again."

He then goes on to say that a very wicked justice called Thomas Howth, with the Lord Mountgarret, resorted to the cathedral church on the following morning, the feast of St. Anne, requesting the priests to have Mass said in her honor. They replied that the bishop had forbidden that celebration except on Sundays. "I discharge you," said Howth, "of obedience to your Bishop in this point, and command you to do as you have done heretofore." This fine action won for him the proud distinction of being called by Bale "a wicked Justice," "a contempter of his prince's earnest commandment," and "a beastly papist."

---

[7]   The territories of Ireland controlled by the English government. — Ed. note.

[8]   Quoted by Ronan, *The Reformation in Dublin*, p. 392.

But over a month later, the city seems to have gone wild with jubilation. The same delicate pen describes what happened, and we shall allow his description to speak for itself. "On Thursday, the last day of August," says the bigoted Bale, "I being absent, the clergy of Kilkenny blasphemously resumed the whole papism.... They rang all the bells in that cathedral, minster, and parish churches; they flung up their caps to the battlements of the great temple, with smilings and laughings most dissolutely; they brought forth their capes, candlesticks, holy water stocks, crosses and censers; they mustered forth in general procession most gorgeously all the town over, with *Sancta Maria, Ora Pro Nobis* and the rest of the Latin Litany. They chattered it, they chanted it with great noise and devotion; they banqueted all the day after, for that they were delivered ... into a warm sun."[9]

[9] Ibid., pp. 402–3.

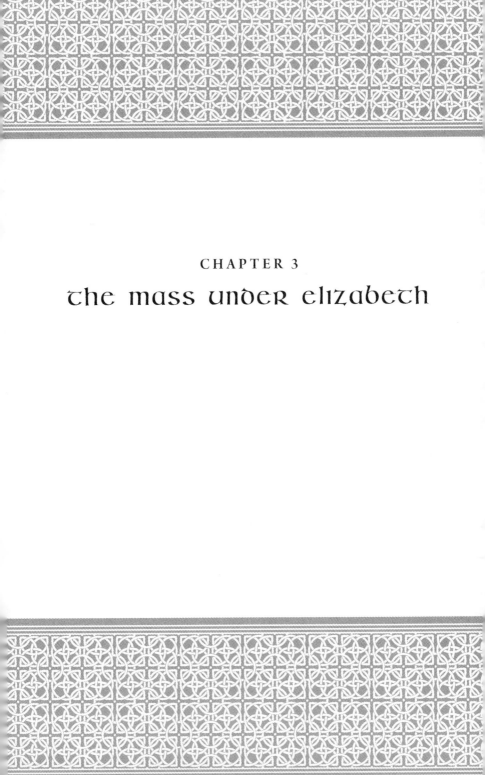

CHAPTER 3

the mass under elizabeth

EDWARD VI DIED ON the sixth of July 1553, and was succeeded by his half-sister Mary, who was crowned on the first of October. On the fifth, Parliament opened, and before its opening, in accordance with ancient customs, she, with all the members of both Houses, assisted at the Mass of the Holy Ghost. Mass was also celebrated in some of the London churches at the request of the congregations, but it was not regularly re-established until the decision of Parliament was promulgated on the twenty-first of December.

England, in the preceding month, was solemnly reconciled to the Holy See by Cardinal Pole, who, a month later, issued a decree in accordance with which the possessors of Church property were not to be disturbed, on ecclesiastical grounds, either then or in the future. This, however, did not wholly satisfy the governing families, who still feared that some attempt might yet be made to restore to the rightful owner the possessions of which the Church had been unjustly deprived during the two preceding reigns. In January 1554, therefore, a comprehensive bill confirmed the legate's decree, and at the same time declared invalid all the statutes promulgated against the papal authority since the twentieth year of Henry VIII.[10] The

---

[10] Pastor, *The History of the Popes,* vol. 13, p. 287.

reconciliation thus fully accomplished was accepted by the heir to the throne, almost the entire governing class, and the vast majority of the people. England was again in union with Rome, altars were restored in the churches, and the Mass was triumphant once more.

There still remained, however, a small number of sincere reforming fanatics who hated every manifestation of Catholicism and, above all, the priests as its living embodiment. Against these enemies Mary now turned all her zeal, and by punishing only for heresy, she allowed the means of escape to those who had grown rich on the property of the Church and who had conformed to the religion of their sovereign merely in order to retain the fruits of successful sacrilege.

In Ireland, Mary's political policy was the same as that of Henry and Edward, but in this country also she did all in her power to wipe out every vestige of the anti-Roman policy of her two predecessors. The Irish monasteries, however, were not reestablished, nor were their lands restored, and owing to this, the Church was, unfortunately, not able to regain her former position in the social and political life of the country.

There was no persecution of Protestants on account of their religion, as some prejudiced historians have falsely asserted, and their number, as a matter of fact, not only in Dublin, but in the whole country, was really insignificant. There were, however, removals from positions to which the occupants had no right. On the twenty-ninth of June 1554, for instance, Staples, bishop of Meath, was deprived of the trust he had so shamefully betrayed. Before the end of the year, Browne of Dublin, Lancaster of Kildare, and Travers of Leighlin were treated in like manner, while Bale of Ossory and Casey of Limerick had already fled beyond the seas.

The Deputy Fitzwalker received special instructions to repair the injuries already wrought by the futile efforts at "reform" and to promote the becoming adornment of the churches. But above all, the great central act of our Faith, the heart and soul of Catholic worship, the head and front of Irish offending, was to be as before. In other words, the adorable Sacrifice of the Mass, which the "reformers" hated and tried to destroy, was to be restored in all its ancient beauty and liturgical splendor.

Hope was strong in Irish hearts for a renewed efflorescence of Catholic worship when the tragic news came that Mary had died in November 1558. She had reigned but five years, and having no children, was succeeded by her half-sister, Elizabeth, whose ascent of the throne was unchallenged. During the reign of her predecessor, Elizabeth had professed attachment to Catholicity and answered Mary's doubts as to her sincerity with the blazing protest: "I pray God that the earth may open and swallow me alive if I be not a true Roman Catholic."

Even after Mary's death, she continued to attend Mass and Vespers as before. Despite all, however, there were still many who maintained that, if not entirely atheist, she was at least anti-Catholic. Her religion was really a matter of expediency, her theology "all words," and its technical terms, as Froude has it, merely "served to vary the vocabulary of her oaths." She soon revealed herself in her true light.

At Christmas, she ordered Oglethorpe, bishop of Carlisle, to omit the elevation of the Sacred Host at Mass, and when he declined to do so, she left the chapel even before the Offertory. But at her coronation on the fifteenth of January, she determined to have her way, and in addition to the omission of the elevation, many changes were introduced into the Adorable Sacrifice. Parliament opened on the twenty-fifth, and a few weeks later diplomatic relations were broken off with the pope. After violent opposition, the bill regarding the royal supremacy was passed, but Elizabeth had to cede the title of Head of the Church, which Mary had never adopted, and accepted instead that of "chief governor of all spiritual and ecclesiastical affairs."

This having been passed and approved, Parliament was pro-
rogued until after Easter, and in the interval, the queen concentrated
her energies on another endeavor. The pope and the Mass were the
two great bugbears, and one having been pushed aside, the other
must be swept away.

Knowing well that she would encounter opposition in Parliament, she resorted to intimidation and imprisoned the bishops of
Lincoln and Winchester in the Tower. Though in the Upper House
there was a majority of only three, the bill for the introduction of the
new liturgy was, nevertheless, passed, and the sublime Sacrifice of
our Faith abolished. On the twenty-fourth of June, the feast of St.
John the Baptist, the new order of things was to come into force, and
the Mass, which had been for a thousand years so intimately associated with the religious and social life of England, was to cease
throughout the length and breadth of the land.

The reader may wonder why so much space is devoted to hap-
penings in England, but it is absolutely necessary to bear these things
in mind in order to be able to trace the religious developments in
Ireland. After Elizabeth's accession, the old order of things continued
as usual, and for three months, the Latin Mass was celebrated in the
Dublin cathedrals. More than a quarter of a year later, Thomas, Earl
of Sussex, a professing Catholic, who restored Catholic worship in
Ireland under Mary, now reluctantly returned in August with orders
from Elizabeth to introduce, in a modified form, the English liturgy.
Some slight beginnings were cautiously made, and a little peaceful
penetration was attempted, but for more than four months longer,
the Catholic ritual was left untouched, and the ancient religion was
the only one recognized by law in Ireland.

On the eleventh of January 1560, Parliament met in Christ
Church, Dublin. No really reliable account has yet been discovered
of the work of this assembly, but there is a well-founded tradition
that the enactments ascribed to it reached the Statute Book by a

trick of James Stanihurst, speaker of the Lower House. Among these, the two most important were the Act of Supremacy and the Act of Uniformity. By the former, the queen was declared, as already in England, supreme governor, not only in purely temporal, but also in spiritual and ecclesiastical matters, and the jurisdiction of the pope was denied. By the Act of Uniformity, the Book of Common Prayer was imposed on all, and the people were commanded to attend Protestant service on all Sundays and holy days under pain of a heavy fine.

This fine was to be changed to imprisonment for life in the case of those that refused for the third time to comply. Moreover, to any priest who declined to use the Protestant Service Book instead of his own Catholic missal, or even dared to speak against it, "or used any other rite of administration of the Sacraments or open prayers," the same severe sentence was to be meted out. Christ's unbloody Sacrifice, in other words, was to be abolished, and according to the Catholic form, His Sacraments were to be administered no more.

But the Irish people were not daunted by this legislation. They fought it with various weapons according to circumstances, and even the women, under great provocation, sometimes resorted to physical force. Not only in the heart of the city wherein this unjust law was enacted, but throughout the entire country wherever it was sought to be enforced, it was met by a vigorous opposition that does honor to the noble character of the Irish race and to their genuine love for the most precious jewel of that Catholic Faith that was preached to them by St. Patrick.

It was one thing to enact laws, but it was quite another to enforce them. There was no machinery for this purpose outside a limited area, and even here the small English garrison, many of whom were Catholics, had very little heart in this heretical work. As a consequence, things went on much as before, the people continued to go to Mass, and ignored the laws that they could not respect.

"Indeed," says Fr. Myles Ronan,[11] "in view of the fact that the very cities and counties that had representatives in Parliament resisted stubbornly the introduction of the new religious service, and that most of the lay peers and gentry clung tenaciously to the Mass, it is humanly improbable that they had anything to do with the passing of those Acts."

Elizabeth's Irish policy, from first to last, had for its objective the political subjugation of Ireland and its complete uniformity with England in religion, language, and customs. The ancient religion must be destroyed. The Irish laws were to be discarded. English dress was to be adopted, and the English language alone should be taught in the schools. The imposition of foreign rule now went hand-in-hand with the imposition of a foreign religion, and this connection on the English side brought about a wonderful union among the Irish. It united not only the native Irish but also the descendants of the colonists and enabled them to offer a splendid resistance to the reformed doctrines. The result was the emergence of a broader and grander idea of nationality in which love of the clan was swallowed up in love of the country. As in Henry's reign Protestantism in Ireland became inseparably bound up with England's interests, in the reign of Elizabeth Catholicism became intimately entwined with Irish aspirations, and in the language itself, Protestant became synonymous with Sasanach.[12]

During the early years of Elizabeth's reign, secular affairs seem to have occupied more of her attention than "reform" matters. She and her advisers were more anxious to maintain their uncertain power in the country than to propagate the new doctrines. They feared a combined Irish and foreign confederation against England, and the chief organizer of this possible combine was the Earl of Kildare, who had

[11] Ronan, *The Reformation in Ireland*, pp. 34–35.
[12] The term *Sasanach* is used to refer to an Englishman. — Ed. note.

refused to abandon the Mass. When the danger had passed, the queen addressed herself to the furtherance of the reform, but her chief difficulty was in procuring a few suitable bishops and clergy-men for important sees and parishes. The infliction of fines for non-attendance at Protestant service was not, for prudential reasons, often insisted on, but whenever the government had power, the law against public Mass was rigorously enforced.

In 1564, an ecclesiastical commission was appointed to ascer-tain how the law regarding attendance at state worship was observed and to compel the people's conscience to accept the Protestant reli-gion. In a letter dated the seventeenth of May 1565, Loftus, nominal archbishop of Armagh, as head of the fifteen commissioners, tells Elizabeth that not only the poor people of the Pale but the very gen-try and nobility had not obeyed her Majesty's commands. The jurors at these sessions of ecclesiastical inquiry were reluctant to give evi-dence against the gentry, but the gentry themselves came forward gladly, and though not under oath, confessed boldly that the vast majority of them had not attended Protestant service but had been going to Mass as if no law against it had been passed.

That was serious enough in the eyes of Loftus, but something more serious still was also elicited. Not only had these educated classes "continually, since the last Parliament, frequented the Mass, and other service and ceremonies inhibited by her Majesty's laws and injunctions," but they had gone so far as to throw open their mansions as Mass-houses whither the Catholic people flocked. They even gave bed and board to the Mass-priests who were forbidden by law to say Mass in a public church. This was done not merely in a chance fashion but by fixed arrangement for each district. Hence the archbishop says that they were "linked in friendship and alliance one with the other," and he thought it would be a good thing to impose "upon everyone of them according to the quality of their several of-fences a good sound fine and sum of money.... And verily in my opinion," he goes on to say, "if they were once brought to some good order and dutiful obedience, somewhat sharply dealt with all now," it would be a great means of bringing "the rest and meaner sort to a godly reformation." Thus it is quite clear that not only the poor denizens of the city and the poor farm laborers in the country but even *"the nobility and chief gentlemen of the English Pale, and the greatest number too"* turned their backs on the Protestant service and clung with all their souls to the Mass.[13]

Sixteen years after Elizabeth's accession, Loftus, now archbishop of Dublin, petitioned Burghley to relieve him of his charge. In doing so, he confesses, as with the rest of the queen's bishops, the failure of the "reform" "amongst this stubborn and obstinate generation." Two years later, Sir Henry Sydney found that the people of Munster "are, for the most part, all papists, and that of the malicioust degree." He complains, moreover, of the ruinous condition of the parish churches, of the scarcity of worthy Protestant clergy, and the want of provision for those that might be called over from England or Scotland to carry on the work.

In 1576, Sir William Drury became president of Munster and hanged four hundred persons in one year. Sent in the same year to suppress a rising of the Connacht Burkes, Sir Nicholas Malby spared neither young nor old and burned all the corn and all the houses. In this manner, by hangings and robbings, by fire and sword, the work of anglicization and evangelization was sought to be pushed forward. But to the one and the other the people of Ireland presented a bold front, and even when robbed of their lands, they still resisted, by every means at their disposal, all attempts to rob them of their Faith.

This vigorous resistance did not weaken with the passage of time, and the regular "reports" sent from this country by the minions of the queen are abundantly sprinkled with choice adjectives that

---

[13] Ronan, *The Reformation in Ireland,* pp. 138, 140.

furnish incontestable proof of the fact. *Papistical* seems to have been held in special affection by these bigoted writers, but it is reinforced at times by such complimentary words as *stubborn, stiff-necked,* and *incorrigible.* All four were, in fact, once joined together in an immortal *crescendo* to describe "the people of the city of Waterford."

Of these, Sir William Drury, writing in the year 1577 to Walsingham, the queen's principal secretary of state, gives a very interesting account that has been justly characterized as one of the most damaging records of the failure of the "reform" in Munster. He breathes vengeance against Louvain where there is, he says, a large number of students from Waterford, "by whom and by the others aforesaid the proud and undutiful inhabiters of this town are so cankered in popery" that he finds it very difficult to describe them. They are, he assures Walsingham, so "undutiful to her Majesty, slandering the gospel publicly as well this side the sea as beyond in England, that they fear not God nor man, and hath their altars, painted images and candlesticks, in derision of the gospel, every day in their Synagogues."[14]

In spite of all his terrorism, and notwithstanding that they acknowledged Elizabeth as head of the state, he has to admit that "Masses infinite they have in their several churches every morning." But what seems to anger him most is that they not only have their Masses in public churches in defiance of the law but that they seem to frequent them "without any fear" whatever. Fired with the zeal of Saul in his most fanatical days, he then glories in the fact that he had "spied them," and being an early riser in pursuance of this lordly work, he arrived one "Sunday at five in the morning and saw them resort out of the churches by heaps."[15]

[14] Quoted by Fr. Ronan, *Reformation in Ireland,* p. 549.
[15] Ibid.

Such fearless loyalty to the Mass must have increased the anger of the savage Drury, who, as with his royal patroness, was working hard not only to de-Irishize but also to de-Catholicize Ireland. In the latter respect, her Irish and English policy was the same. In England, as we have said, the work of de-Catholicization meant not only to break with the pope but also to abolish the Mass. Cecil and his robber gang knew well that as long as people demanded the Mass, they would also demand the priest, and in order that they could rest secure in their stolen Church lands, their selfish, sordid aim was to persuade the people that the priests were not indispensable.[16]

But in this matter, by no reasoning whatever, could the Irish people be persuaded. Here, too, hatred of the Mass for its own sake, as the essence of Catholicity, was very much in evidence, as well as hatred of the priest, not only as the minister of that Sacrifice, but also as the foundation of the whole structure of the Church, which the reformers were out to destroy. Persecution, therefore, waxed more intense as time went on, till it seemed as if all the fury of Hell had been at last let loose against every thing and every person having any connection whatever with the Mass.

Being the celebrants of what is, undoubtedly, the greatest action on earth, bishops and priests were, of course, the prime offenders and, consequently, the chief objects of attack. Every law passed against them was, therefore, a blow struck not only at the religion that the Irish Catholics professed but also against the Mass, which is the most distinctive feature of that religion. The second Book of Common Prayer that Elizabeth wished to force on Ireland, with the ritual of the first that was hated by the colonists, denied the sacrificial character of the Mass as derogatory to the great Sacrifice of the Cross. But the Irish loved this sacramental Sacrifice not only as a true sacrifice in itself, not only as a

---

[16] Hollis, *The Monstrous Regiment*, p. 37.

representation, but as a real re-presentation and perfect image of all that occurred on Calvary when Christ died for the salvation of the human race. The Englishman's hatred of the Mass was pitted against the Irishman's love of it. The Irishman's love of it was reflected in his love for the priest, and the history of our country proves abundantly that this twin-love was stronger than death.

These things must be constantly borne in mind throughout the reading of these pages in order to see clearly the reason of the fierce pursuit of priests, and of the frightful sufferings to which they were subjected when captured. In August 1579, at Kilmallock, a strong garrison town, Dr. Patrick O'Hely of the Franciscan Order, bishop of Mayo, and a brother Franciscan named Fr. Conor O'Rourke fell into the hands of the savage Drury, who, two years previously, had complained of "Masses infinite" being attended by crowds of people "without any fear." Having no love for priests, he was well-known to have a special antipathy to friars, and on this occasion, two of the terrible tribe were brought before him. Interrogated as to their character, they confessed boldly that they had been sent by Pope Gregory XIII and that their only business was to advance the Catholic religion and to save souls. As a result, they received the full measure of his hatred, and the frequent reward of their calling. Condemning them to the rack, he had needles thrust under their nails, and their legs and arms broken with hammers. After this, they were hanged upon a tree, where their bodies were left suspended for four days as targets for the bullets of the soldiers. But in fulfillment of the prophecy that the bishop had uttered on his way to execution, Drury died fourteen days later, in great agony, in the city of "Masses infinite without any fear."

On the twenty-ninth of June, Marmaduke Middleton, the Protestant bishop of Waterford and Lismore, writing to Walsingham, gives a description[17] of the state of his diocese, which opens with this sweeping sentence: "Such is the miserable state of this wretched City (Waterford) that all things are done contrary to the sacred word and blessed will of the Lord." "The Gospel of God," he continues, "is utterly abhorred — the church, in time of divine service, of all lands eschewed.... The sacraments contemned and refused — Massing in every corner — No burial of the dead according to the Book of Common Prayer, but buried in their houses with dirges and afterwards cast into the ground like dogs — Rome runners and Friars maintained amongst them — Public wearing of beads and praying upon the same — worshipping of images and setting them openly in their street doors, with ornaments and deckings. Ringing of bells and praying for the dead, and dressing their graves divers times in the year with flower pots and wax candles." Bearing in mind the character of Elizabeth, one can hardly repress a smile on reading the next of this long catalogue of "sins": "No marriage agreeing with God's law and Her Majesty's proceeding." But our hearts swell with pride when we read immediately afterwards that "they marry in houses with Masses." Of all this and more the poor Protestant bishop had to complain regarding the "stiffnecked, stubborn, papistical and incorrigible people of the City of Waterford." It was indeed bad enough to have the men so shockingly recalcitrant, but it must have almost broken his tender heart to have to complain of the women. Having told us that "the windows and the walls of the churches are full of images," and saying, "They will not deface them, and I dare not for fear of a tumult," he adds with a sigh that we can almost hear through the centuries, "None of the women do come either to service or sermons." Surely there must have been something strangely wrong in this southern city, and, indeed, in the entire province, when the most

[17] Quoted by Egan, *Waterford*, pp. 154–55.

strenuous attempts at "reformation" made by the highest dignitaries in Church and state had proved so utterly abortive.

But in this valuable letter there is another sentence that throws a bright light on the union that existed between priests and people in their gallant fight for the Faith of their fathers. "There is," the bishop says, "no difference betwixt the Clergy and laity here, for they have joined together to prevent Her Majesty's Most Godly proceeding." The Mass was the focus of the enemy's hatred, and it was also the magnet of the people's devotion. Masses infinite in churches, Masses in houses, Masses in every corner — these were the "crimes" with which the people of this country were charged. They are offenses in which we should glory, and the denunciations leveled against the devoted men and women who lived in the "dark and evil days" of three hundred years[18] ago are as a splendid eulogy of their imperishable loyalty, which should be a stimulus to us to love and cherish the Mass in the bright and happy days that now are ours.

---

[18] At the time of the 1933 publication. Over four hundred years at the publication of this edition. — Ed. note.

CHAPTER 4

the mass under
elizabeth (continued)

Almost half of Elizabeth's reign was over, and she had made very little progress in Ireland in the establishment of the new religion or the abolition of the ancient Mass. The Acts of Supremacy and Uniformity had indeed been passed in the Parliament of Ireland, and the pope's claim of spiritual jurisdiction had been made treasonable. But the Irish people were as attached to the pope as ever. Irish bishops and lords had sent him a declaration of their loyalty and had dispatched agents not only to Paris and Madrid but also to Rome asking for help to carry on a religious war for the recovery of their churches, then mostly in ruins, and for freedom of public worship.

All this activity abroad culminated in the disastrous expedition of James Fitzmaurice, one of the bravest and noblest Irishmen that ever lived. The force that had been sent to the assistance of the Desmonds took up their position in Dún-an-óir, the Golden Fort, an ancient castle standing on a small promontory jutting out into Smerwick Bay and connected with the mainland by a narrow strip of land. Though the eight hundred troops, mostly Spaniards and Italians, were well armed and provisioned, the fortress was delivered up, on the morning of the third day of the siege, by San Josepho, the Spanish leader, and a terrible massacre followed.

It is not, however, on this shameless massacre that we now wish to dwell but rather on the fate of a few of those who were in the fort when it was given up to Lord Deputy Grey de Wilton. These are Fr. Laurence Moore, an Irish gentleman named Plunkett, who acted as interpreter, and William Walsh, an Englishman and also a soldier, who, before the slaughter began, had been handed over to the lord deputy and reserved for special punishment. The usual inducements were, of course, held out to them if they would only acknowledge the queen as head of the Church. But rejecting every temptation, their invariable answer was that they were Catholics and determined to live or, if necessary, prepared to die in defense of their Faith.

All efforts to change them having failed, they were led off to the forge of an iron-smith where their arms and legs were broken in three different parts. The priest, however, was subjected to an additional torture, which shows, as nothing else could, the devilish hatred that burned in so many "reformed" hearts at the time against the minister and the Sacrament of the Altar. The thumbs and forefingers of the priest were cut off because, as his executioners said, they had been so often employed in the *consecration of the Eucharist* and had *touched it*. All that night and the following day they bore their torments with Christlike patience. At length, hanged and afterwards cut in pieces, they received the martyrs' crown on the feast of St. Martin 1580.[19]

At this time a priest, who had been for about twenty-five years professor of philosophy at the University of Louvain, was teaching canon and civil law in Rheims. This priest, Dermot O'Hurley, having been called to Rome, learned that he had been appointed to the See of Cashel by Gregory XIII, was consecrated archbishop on the eleventh of September 1581, and received the pallium on the twenty-seventh of November.

We can easily imagine his feelings at this moment as he thought of the land where so much awaited him. Of material warfare in

[19]   O'Rourke, *The Battle of the Faith in Ireland*, p. 26.

Ireland there was now no talk of renewal, but the spiritual warfare had to be continued. Bishops had to be provided for those who were still waging such a heroic fight for their Faith, yet it was hard to run the gauntlet and to get safe to the Irish shore. The queen's ships scoured the turbulent seas and government spies were watching sharply at every port. "Rome-runners" were a precious capture, and papal bulls brought a rich reward, while he who bore them was marked guilty of high treason, and the penalty was imprisonment with death.

The newly consecrated archbishop was well aware of all this, yet, though now nearly sixty years of age, never once did he falter. Fortified by the blessing of him who had already more than once generously helped his Irish children, he would go — he and many another in future years — drawn by the thought of hungry souls that were longing for the food of God's Word, and of loving hearts that were yearning for the Sacraments and the Mass.

Disguised probably as a seaman, he landed safe at Skerries in North Dublin and, accompanied by a faithful sailor, pushed on by land to Drogheda. Hoping to be able to pick them up again at Waterford, he confided a box containing the papal bulls of his appointment, his episcopal robes, vestments, pallium, pyxes, chalice, and the rest of his belongings to the care of the captain of a merchant ship. The merchant ship was captured, and the episcopal belongings confiscated. Later on, having spent some days with his own flock, he found himself in Dublin on the seventh of October 1583, and was at once thrown into a dark and filthy dungeon.

Kept there till the Holy Thursday of the following year, as if by a perverted instinct of diabolical hatred, on this day of burning memories connected with the Sacrament of Love, he was brought before the two lords justices, Adam Loftus, archbishop of Dublin, and Sir Henry Wallop, treasurer of war. Promised pardon if he would deny the spiritual authority of the pope and take the Oath of Supremacy, he boldly refused. Thrown on the ground and tied to the trunk of a tree, he was then submitted to punishment of the most exquisite cruelty. Only some groans were forced from him, mingled with the sweet prayer of solace: "Jesus, Son of David, have mercy on me."

Tried later by pitch and fire, with flesh melting and bones exposed, he was still undefeated. Having tortured his body, they wished to break his spirit. But they failed. No compromising confession, no coveted recantation could they force from his unconquerable soul. Baffled in their aim and fearful that they had gone too far, they flung him back into prison. Lest they should be robbed of the joy of seeing him die in the way they intended, restoratives were applied, and after a couple of weeks, he was again able to meet his judges.

Blandishments were now tried, promises of ecclesiastical promotion, and the gracious favor of the queen. But all to no purpose. At last, a brilliant idea struck the minds of the lords justices, and they hastened to put it into execution. Fearing the issue of a public trial, they sought the permission of her Majesty to proceed against him by martial law. Elizabeth at length gave her sanction, and O'Hurley was sentenced to be hanged on the gallows outside the city. And so, on a certain summer morning at dawn, the aged archbishop of Cashel was bundled into a cart in the castle yard. Out through the postern gate, surrounded by armed soldiers, the cart was drawn, then through streets and across fields to Gallows Green, where Merrion Row and Ely Place now meet. Here, true to the Faith to the last, and with the words "I am a priest anointed and also a bishop" on his lips, he was hanged on the gibbet on Friday the twentieth of June 1584.

The murder of Dr. Dermot O'Hurley was meant to strike terror into all the "Rome-runners" and Mass-priests then in Ireland. But in spite of every punishment for obstinacy and every inducement to apostasy, the ministers of Christ could not be cowed but remained exasperatingly firm. Some months later, therefore, in this same year, an order was issued having for its object their total extermination. In virtue of this edict, all the priests found in the kingdom were declared, by the very fact, to be guilty of high treason, condemned to be hanged, cut down while yet alive, disemboweled, burned, and beheaded.

The surest way to expel the Mass was to destroy the priests. But though hunted like wild beasts, imprisoned and starved, tortured and executed, they could not, nevertheless, be so easily exterminated. By careful hiding and often by monetary bribes, they were able to say Mass now and then, in private rooms and decent outhouses, for the flocks that were previously notified of the meeting place and came to confess and receive the Bread of Life. Sometimes, even very daring spirits were found, like Dame Eleanor Birmingham, the widow of Bartholomew Baal or Ball, who befriended priests on every occasion and whose career deserves more than a mere passing reference.

Living in Dublin, she managed to hear Mass on all feast days, and as with St. Francis of Assisi, "thought it almost a crime" not to assist at it every day, if at all possible. That she might the more surely achieve this and satisfy her intense devotion, she succeeded in keeping a priest constantly in her house. Suspicion having at last fallen upon her, soldiers were sent in the early morning and found the priest at the altar offering up the Holy Sacrifice. The chalice, paten, and other sacred things were at once seized by these sacrilegious intruders, and the priest, with this devoted lady, hurried away. Both were flung into prison, but she, smoothing the way with money, was after some time set free. Leading the same life as before, and devoted as ever to the Mass, she was again cast into prison by her false son, Walter, who had betrayed Hurley. There she peacefully passed away in her dungeon, in the same year in which the noble archbishop perished on the gallows.

The following year is intimately associated with the name of one priest whose life might be woven a story as thrilling as any romance. It was Easter Saturday 1585. In the jail of Clonmel had lain, for more than twelve months, a very holy priest, once chaplain to Gerald, the lately murdered Earl of Desmond. In the town was a well-known man, named Victor White, who was on friendly terms with the governor of the jail. Partly owing to this and the tactful use of a generous bribe, White obtained the favor of having the priest to spend this particular night and the following morning with himself and his family. Thus, he lovingly and longingly thought that not only they but also all the Catholics of the district would have the great joy of celebrating the feast of the Resurrection with Confession, Communion, and Mass.

Sometime after the bargain had been concluded, the president of Munster, Sir John Norris, rode unexpectedly into town. Fearing the priest might be missed and himself punished, the crafty governor, when night had fallen, sought out the president. Pretending that he had liberated the priest to entrap the Catholics, he told Norris where, on the following morning, he could catch Fr. Maurice Kinrechtin offering up Mass in presence of the principal men of the place. Accordingly, before the Easter sun had risen on the morrow, the mansion of Victor White was broken into by a body of soldiers with the president of Munster at their head.

Rushing everywhere, they created indescribable confusion. Women and children fled in all directions, escaping by back doors and windows. Every corner was searched, but no trace could be found of the priest who, not having begun Mass, had secretly escaped and was now safely hidden in a heap of straw outside. Even here, much prodding of pikes and swords failed to evoke even a groan from the wounded fugitive. At last, disappointed and infuriated, White was threatened with confiscation of his property and even death if he did not tell them of the hiding place of the priest. Failing to move him in the least, they bound him hand and foot and, taking him away, flung him into prison. After a short time, he was told that he would receive the supreme penalty of the law if before a certain day the audacious violator of her Majesty's commands had not delivered himself into their hands.

Hearing of his friend's danger, and knowing well the punishment that awaited himself, Fr. Maurice at once left his refuge in the country, made his way back to Clonmel, where, surrendering himself into the hands of the authorities, he was loaded with chains and flung into a noisome dungeon. During his trial, threats and promises were prodigally used, but he would neither renounce the Faith nor acknowledge the queen. Firm as a mighty rock lashed by raging surf, no threat however violent, no punishment however awful, could draw from him even one word that might lead to the discovery of those who had at any time assisted at his Masses or received from him the Sacraments.

Condemned at last to die, he was dragged on a hurdle at the horse's tail to the scaffold, beneath whose shadow he spoke to the people and exhorted them to be true to the Faith to the end. While still half alive, he was taken down from the gallows. Partly by entreaties and partly by bribes, the quartering of his body was prevented. But while the rest of his remains were buried in the Franciscan church in the town, his head was cut off and put on a stake above the market cross on the thirtieth of April 1585.

The head on the stake, instead of inspiring terror, only increased devotion. Day after day the people gathered round it, and its mute lips to them spoke words of hope that kept alive in their souls the flame of devotion to the Sacrifice of the Mass.

Years rolled slowly by. Deputies came and planned; they planned and plotted; they plotted and passed away. But always went on the struggle for homes and altars, which revealed again and again superb courage and splendid loyalty. At last, Hugh O'Neill won his great victory at the Yellow Ford in 1598, and a year later a similar triumph was achieved, on the same feast, by Aodh Ruadh O'Donnell.

Though not the first of Irish leaders, Red Hugh was certainly the most captivating and romantic of Irish princes. His fame is still fresh and bright after the passage of more than three hundred years;[20] his name still lives in song and story, and his loyalty to the Mass is remembered as a prominent feature in his whole life. His biographer, Lewy

[20] Now more than four hundred years. — Ed. note.

51

O'Clery, tells us that he kept a priest constantly with him "to offer Mass and the pure mysterious Sacrifice of the Body and Blood of Christ." Whenever he set out on a journey or a hosting, or whenever threatened with any danger, his invariable practice was to observe a fast, confess his sins, assist at Mass, and receive Holy Communion. He certainly was in grave danger in the late summer of 1599, and while Hugh O'Neill was pushing forward by forced marches to his aid, despite the fact that his army was inferior in numbers to that of the enemy, he resolved not to wait but to give battle to the English.

It was the fourteenth of August, the eve of the feast of the Assumption of the Blessed Virgin, familiarly known in Ireland as "Lady Day in Harvest." On this day, the whole army fasted, and on the following morning, the feast itself, all assisted at Mass, while O'Donnell and the chief officers received Holy Communion, "with great reverence for the Lord Jesus Christ and His Holy Mother." After Mass, the soldiers repaired to their tents to take some food and to prepare for the great labor of the day. Then they went forth with great joy, hoping in their hearts that the God Who died for them would be with them in the fight.

"Dauntless Red Hugh," sword in hand, now addressed his troops, and his voice, "like that of a silver trumpet," rolled over their heads in an impassioned strain of wonderful eloquence that must have fired their inmost souls. They were fighting, he said, for their homes and their altars, against the paid soldiers of a heretic queen. On their side were right and justice, on the English injustice and robbery. They must strike and conquer, or rot in prison and in chains. They should not be frightened by the number of the enemy, nor the strangeness of their arms. Let them put their trust in God, and they would surely win. He who fell in the battle would fall gloriously, fighting for liberty. His deeds would never be forgotten, and his name would be remembered for ever. He who survived would be pointed out everywhere as the companion of O'Donnell and the defender of his country. In the church, the people would make room for him, and as he moved toward the altar, looking at him with pride, they would whisper to each other and say, "That hero fought at Dunaveeragh."

Even from this sketchy résumé, and in a cold translation, one can easily imagine the effect that the passionate Irish words must have had on the Irish troops. With glowing minds and burning hearts, they disposed themselves for the battle, which began at four o'clock in the afternoon. The English fought with desperate valor, and Clifford bravely led his men, but trying to rally them in flight, he perished gallantly, and ere the sun went down, victory had perched on the Irish banners. Only about 240 had fallen on the Irish side, and the survivors knew well "that it was not by force of arms they had gained the victory" but by the prayers of O'Donnell, by the protection of the Blessed Virgin, and above all, by the power of the Mass.

More than a year later occurred an event that testifies in a very striking manner to the bitter hatred of the Irish people for the Protestant worship and their intense loyalty to the Mass. Twenty years previously, the young Earl of Desmond, when but a mere child of seven, had been delivered up as a hostage to Sir William Drury, the lord justice. After two or three years in his charge, he was sent to London to spend seventeen years in the hands of English jailers and under the tutelage of the apostate Miler Magrath. The savage Carew, who was still president of Munster, thought that the time had at length arrived when the youthful James Fitzgerald could be released from the Tower and sent across to Ireland, where his presence would be sure to create some division in the Irish forces and thus further English interests.

His approaching visit was proclaimed far and wide, and a herald, wearing the Desmond livery, was sent through the country announcing the glad tidings. When all was ready and everyone keenly expectant, the young Earl, landing at Youghal in October 1600, reached Kilmallock soon after, on a Saturday evening. At his entry into the town, he was met by a mighty concourse of people. The streets were thronged, windows were crowded, and doors choked. The very gutters and roofs of the houses swarmed with men and women. It seemed as if they were welcoming one specially sent by God to be their comfort and joy, the desired of their hearts and souls. They shouted and cheered, they were delirious with delight, throwing upon him wheat and salt as a token of hearty welcome and a prediction of peace and plenty. The soldiers with difficulty made a narrow lane for him as he walked through the street, and were it not for this guard the people would have unwittingly done him bodily harm in the ecstasy of their jubilation.

Night passed and morning dawned. It was Sunday, and the crowds were still around. All were anxious to see and greet him once more. As he came forth from his lodging, the soldiers closed around him. A wild burst of cheering shook the air, but it soon died away in a groan when, to the horror of the people, all marched in the direction of the Protestant church. By every means in their power, they tried to prevent the advance of the Earl, but all in vain. When service was over, he was met with the fierce anger and awful scowls of his countrymen and women. He had cut them to the very soul by his conduct, and though he was scarcely to blame, they would hear of no excuse. The night before, they would have gladly poured out their hearts' blood for him, but now they hooted and spat upon him because he had turned his back on the Faith for which his kinsmen had so gallantly fought, and upon the priests and the Mass that they had so splendidly defended.

What the people thought then of the Mass and of the priest may be gathered from two very striking events that happened about this time. The first is associated with the name of one whose poetic nature gave him a great insight into the truth of things and whose Catholic Faith taught him the value of the most precious treasure of our religion. Fearghal Óg Mac-a-Ward had occasion to visit Reformation Scotland and there made one of his religious poems in which real sadness mingles with genuine beauty. Pouring out his heart, he bewails his loss of the sacred opportunities of home and betrays his ardent longing for Communion and for Mass. How sad and yet how stirring it is to hear him telling that "in this bright-flowered land of shining fields I receive not the Lord's Body. By my art, I swear," he says, "I was deceived, *and though I owned all Alba … better were one Mass.*"[21]

This phrase should live forever in Irish hearts. It was the expression of our forefathers' estimation of the Mass in those days of unrelenting persecution, and what they thought of the priest may be gathered from the following fact. Hearing that there was a priest among the Irish soldiers defending the castle of Cloghan, Captain George Flower, commander of the English forces, hastened to assault it. Meeting with a stubborn resistance, he threatened to hang in their sight Donnell Dorrogh, the brother of their commander, if they did not surrender. Nevertheless, to save the priest, they obstinately refused, and in consequence, the brother of their leader was hanged before their eyes.

Four days later, having got away the priest in safety, the garrison surrendered as prisoners of war. Sir George Carew, who never showed mercy to priests, having recorded this fact, adds, "I do relate this event to the end (that) the reader may more clearly see in what reverence and estimation these ignorant superstitious Irish do hold a Popish priest, in regard of whose safety, the commander was content to suffer his brother to perish." In the light of faith, the "ignorant" Irish saw in the priest the image of Jesus, because upon the faculties of his soul is imprinted the character of the priesthood of Christ. Beyond this they also saw the relation of daily companionship with Our Lord, and that other of intimate and vital contact with Him in the Sacrifice of the Mass, which was the luminous center of their love as it was the great object of the reformers' hate.

The religious persecution in Ireland during Elizabeth's reign produced a rich crop of martyrs amounting to about *two hundred* or more. Besides these were many confessors, who suffered imprisonment in

---

[21] de Blácam, *Gaelic Literature Surveyed*, p. 138.

filthy dungeons and tortures of exquisite cruelty that often hastened their death. While many of these were laymen, the great majority were priests who were hated with special malignity as the ministers of the Adorable Sacrifice, and among the brave intrepid band are to be found no less than *fourteen* bishops.[22] On one occasion, soldiers made a sudden attack on the Cistercian monastery of St. Mary's at Nenay, Co. Limerick, and slew forty monks and their abbot in the very church before the Blessed Sacrament. Even as late as the last year but one of Elizabeth's reign, two and forty priests were drowned by treachery in the sea. Others were dragged from the altar while saying Mass, while many were slain within the sanctuary itself.

Perhaps the thought of these also mingled with the many unhappy things that are said to have disturbed the peace of the last months of the queen's life. Looking back on her long sway of five and forty years, recalling at least her last few years of Irish government, she must have felt that in many things she had succeeded. The Spanish-Irish combination at Kinsale had been broken; Red Hugh had died in Spain pleading without effect the cause of Ireland; nearly all the Ulster chiefs had submitted; the great Hugh O'Neill himself had retired to the remote fastnesses of Tirowen, and after four centuries and a half, the political conquest of Ireland had been practically achieved. But she must have felt also in the bitterness of her heart that in one great thing, the greatest thing of all — the spiritual conquest of the Irish soul by the rejection of the pope and the expulsion of the Mass — she had absolutely and miserably failed.

---

[22]   O'Rourke, *The Battle of the Faith in Ireland*, p. 24.

CHAPTER 5

The mass under James 1

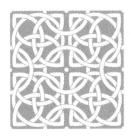

Mountjoy[23] heard of Elizabeth's death at Mellifont, Co. Louth. There he was awaiting the arrival of Hugh O'Neill, who, after his nine years' war against all the power of England, thinking that the queen was still alive, now tendered his submission to her representative on the twenty-ninth of March 1603. Some days later, both arrived in Dublin, where O'Neill learned the truth and is said to have wept tears of rage at the manner in which he had been tricked by the deputy. But tears of joy fell and cries of delight echoed through all the land when the news spread that the arch-persecutor of the Faith had at last passed away.

Strong in the hope that her successor, James I, would grant freedom of worship and allow them once more to assist at Mass openly, the Catholics took peaceful possession of their churches in Waterford, Cashel, Cork, Limerick, and indeed throughout a great part of Munster. Having "reconciled" them by legitimate authority, they enthroned their eucharistic God again on the altars and gathered round Him in the mornings to assist at the Adorable Sacrifice with the same fervor that they had displayed in the days of religious freedom, fifty years before.

[23]   Charles Blount, First Earl of Devonshire, Lord Mountjoy, lord deputy of Ireland. — Ed. note.

So great was the intensity of Catholic feeling that in some places were held great processions of the Blessed Sacrament. In Cork and Waterford, especially, these spontaneous outpourings of devotion were marked by incidents that move us deeply, even now, after the passage of more than three hundred years.[24] In Waterford, all the inhabitants joined, and while tears coursed down their cheeks, they cried out that, since they had seen "their heavenly King, Christ our Lord" borne in triumph once more through their streets, they were ready to face anything, even death itself.

In Cork, a teacher of Latin named Eugene (or Owen) MacRedmond, voiced the sentiments of many a heart. On seeing Our Lord borne in solemn state through the city, surrounded by all the people, he was transported out of himself. In an ecstatic exaltation of spirit, looking up to heaven, he flung out his arms and, as if inspired, "prayed God never to permit Cork to want the power to preserve so happy, holy, and divine a custom." His prayer has been heard, and, thank God, Cork is no stranger today to the grace-laden joy of eucharistic processions.

Never was witnessed such an outburst of devotion. In Wexford and Kilkenny, Carrick and Cashel, Ross and Fethard, and other places the sacred edifices that had been defiled by the heretics were once more purified, altars were restored, sermons were preached, *Te Deums* were sung, bells rang out in gladness, and morning after morning worshipful crowds assisted at Mass. Our eucharistic God had again come unto His own, and His own received Him with demonstrations of loyalty that were like the lavish radiance of sunshine after the violent wreckings of a wintry storm.

Mountjoy soon heard the startling news of this sudden outburst of faith and was indignant at the boldness of the towns that had "set up the public exercise of the Popish worship." "If they did not desist,"

[24] More than four hundred years now. — Ed. note.

he continued, "from … the celebration of the Mass, he would think them fit to be prosecuted with the avenging sword of his Majesty's forces." Setting out at once for the south, he appeared before Waterford with a formidable army, which was refused admission. At Cork, he met with still more resistance and pronounced it to be the most insolent city of all. Having finally effected an entrance, he vented his heretical rage by the public execution of MacRedmond for his splendid exhibition of faith on the occasion of the eucharistic procession.

In 1604, Mountjoy was succeeded by Sir Arthur Chichester. The new deputy started his regime by a series of proclamations in which, among other things, he forbade the carrying of arms by the native Irish. After this precautionary preliminary, he proceeded to put the religious laws in force in districts in Ulster where nothing of the kind had ever been attempted before. Being now secure upon the throne, King James retracted all his previous promises of toleration, and to the horror of the Catholics, his proclamation of the fourth of July 1605, published in Dublin on the twenty-eighth of September, was made to say: "It hath seemed proper to us to proclaim, and we hereby make known to our subjects in Ireland, that no toleration shall ever be granted by us. This we do for the purpose of cutting off all hope that any other religion shall be allowed, save that which is consonant to the laws and statutes of this realm."

The Acts of Supremacy and Uniformity were revived, and Catholics who absented themselves from Protestant service on Sundays or festivals were to be fined or imprisoned, and all priests were required, under penalty of death, to withdraw from the kingdom before the tenth of December. After this date, should any persons receive them into their houses, or support them, or hold converse with them, or not denounce them to the tribunals, they were to be hanged at their own doors. Bands of soldiers were scattered through the country. They were to be seen on the roads and in the fields. Entering into private houses, they seized whatever they liked and executed whomsoever they pleased. Dublin, perhaps, suffered most from the new reign of terror. Many of its leading citizens were proud to pay the penalty of the law in heavy fines, as well as imprisonment, and throughout the country, where nearly all were Catholics, the people scorned to attend heretical worship and gloried in the name of "recusants."

In the last week but one of May 1606 was published another edict in virtue of which, says James White, vicar-apostolic of Waterford and Lismore, "all priests who would be detected, should, without any subterfuge or further trial, be hanged from the first tree or gallows that should present itself." In the same letter to the eminent historian Cardinal Baronius, he instances a case in which three Catholics were arrested. Merely suspecting them to be priests, they "were instantly put to death" by the soldiers. As a matter of fact, he adds, "one of them was, indeed, a priest, the other two were certainly laymen."

Thus perished the hopes of the Catholics who still, in the teeth of every difficulty, continued to practice their religion and assist at Mass whenever an opportunity presented itself. The violence of the persecution knew no bounds, and, says Dominic de Rosario, "The priests of the people were made to suffer, and those who stood by them became participators of their sorrows." Of this we have a striking proof in the case of one of the greatest heroes of the time, whose ardor for the Faith was so abundantly manifested during the reconciliation of churches in the previous reign that he won the proud distinction of being imprisoned in Dublin Castle. Even after his release, Sir John Burke of Brittas continued to display the same zeal for Mass as before, often walking long distances to assist at it. At a very early hour on Rosary Sunday of 1607, his castle at Brittas, about eight miles south of Limerick, was surrounded by a body of cavalry, just as the priest was preparing to offer up the Divine Victim on the altar.

On seeing the soldiers, the people, who were coming from all sides, dispersed, while brave Sir John and his devoted chaplain, Fr.

John Clancy, betook themselves with the sacred vessels to the tower. Though closely besieged for several days, they succeeded in escaping separately, but after many hardships, Sir John, having carefully concealed the sacred vessels, was captured at Carrick. Conveyed to the queen city of the Shannon by a troop of horse, he was put upon his trial, condemned to death, and executed. The remains of this defender of the Faith and lover of the Mass were buried in St. John's, Limerick, five days before Christmas.

Three months previously, the Earls O'Neill and O'Donnell with others, about a hundred persons in all, breaking through the nets of the conspirators, had sailed away quietly from Lough Swilly. Passing through France and Belgium, they were received in Rome with the greatest pomp and ceremony by Paul V, who ever afterwards was to them a father and a friend. He knew well that even within their own estates the celebration of Mass had been forbidden, and availed himself of every possible occasion on which to show his appreciation of the sterling loyalty of the princely exiles to the Faith, in spite of all their sufferings. By his orders they were given "the best place in the church" at the canonization of St. Francisca, on the Thursday preceding Trinity Sunday of the year 1608. On the feast of Corpus Christi also, the Holy Father "ordained that the chiefest of the Irish exiles should alone carry the canopy over him, which eight of them accordingly did." This was the first time that such a distinction was accorded to the Irish, but in these and other ways, the Vicar of Christ wished to show his profound respect for those whom he regarded as defenders of the Faith and lovers of the Mass.

From a *relatio* made in 1609 by Dr. Kearney, archbishop of Cashel, we learn many interesting things of the life of the priests at this time. When persecution pressed and the soldiers were in pursuit, the ministers of Christ fled to secret places, but when it relaxed, they gradually appeared again in public. They went about dressed like ordinary seculars, not stopping long in any one place, but passing

from house to house, "even in the cities and towns." Under cover of
darkness, they transferred the sacred vestments from place to place,
gave exhortations to the people, administered Confirmation, and
celebrated Mass. The heretics were ever on the watch for those that
assisted at the Adorable Sacrifice, while they inflicted fines on those
who absented themselves from Protestant service. They forbade the
use of chapels and flung into prison not only those who favored the
priests but even those that refused to persecute and deliver them up.

The judges, on their circuits, were accompanied by wicked and
desperate men, and the very sessions for murder and other crimes
were held in monasteries and churches. But love is daring as well as
inventive, and so, in the midst of relentless persecution and destruction, the priests and people found places in which to offer up the
great eucharistic Sacrifice. This splendid obstinacy greatly irritated
Chichester, who, writing to the secretary of the Council in England
on the eleventh of May 1610, expressed a longing for greater powers
of punishment. He complained of the liberty of the Catholics in the
exercise of their religion, from which, he adds, in an immortal phrase,
"they cannot restrain them without slaughter or the gallows for
which they have neither law nor warrant."

After this significant hint, he goes on to state that his agents had
quite recently apprehended a priest and then describes the manner in
which this great deed was accomplished at Multyfarnham, in County
Westmeath. Having disguised themselves, they watched carefully and
pounced upon the priest after he had said Mass and bore him away.
Those who had assisted at the Holy Sacrifice gave the alarm, "the
country rose and rescued him from the parties employed, and hurt
them in sundry places." We must pause to admire the delicate way in
which he describes their castigation, and, immediately afterwards, to
emphasize the terrible wickedness of the rescuers, he notes that they
did all this "not-withstanding they showed them his (the Lord Deputy's) warrant, and told them he (the priest) was a proclaimed traitor."

We can easily imagine the just contempt with which these brave Catholics must have treated both the warrant and the words. Not once, nor twice, but many a time during this sad and trying period, our gallant forefathers showed that they were not afraid to join issue, even with well-armed soldiers, in fearless loyalty to the daring "traitors" that were ever ready to risk their liberty and their lives in order to comfort and strengthen their followers by offering up for them the unbloody Sacrifice of Christ.

The disconsolate deputy must have continued to brood over this awful condition of things. He tried hard to find a remedy. A few days later, he sent another letter to the same person, praying for "a commission for the adjudging and execution of *Pirates* and *Priests*, who vex and disturb the Kingdom more than can be understood by others than them that feel it."

This must have had some effect, for, in the following year, 1611, arrived in Ireland a certain bishop, named Knox, who was entrusted with full powers to tear up popery by the roots and to sweep away every trace of Catholicism. Vowing that he would punish "the obstinacy of these wicked papists, and make them curse the Pope," this fiery Scotsman set to work with a will. Bands of informers, perjurors, and murderers swooped down, like ravenous birds of prey, on almost every city, town, and village in Ireland, while the bishop himself went about with a suite of puritanical followers, and whoever fell into their hands had little chance of escape from torments and death. Every means was tried to force Catholics to attend the heretical conventicles. Refusal was punished with fine or imprisonment. Some were robbed of their goods; others were driven into exile; and others were led to the scaffold. Schools were broken up, books torn, and teachers expelled. Priests were sought out to be robbed of their chalices and patens and to be put to death. But the pope was never cursed, and the Mass was still said.

Owing to this terrible and widespread persecution, Dr. Eugene Matthews (MacMahon), before setting out from Rome in the summer of this year, petitioned the reigning pontiff for a very special favor, which was most graciously granted for his See of Dublin. Having stated that "all the churches" in Ireland were "either destroyed by the late persecutions or occupied by the heretics" and that "it is nowise allowed to offer up there the Holy Sacrifice in public, but only in private houses, or in orchards, or in caverns," he requested the Holy Father to permit him "the use of a privileged portable altar, and should one such privileged altar be broken or lost in any way, that he might consecrate another with the same indulgences and privileges."

This great archbishop, Dr. Matthews, was constantly pursued by his enemies and had some hairbreadth escapes. The house in which he was hiding was, on one occasion, surrounded and searched by the priest-hunters, but he, with another priest, his companion, escaped through the attic windows, stole along the roofs of the adjoining houses, descended in some unknown way, and succeeded in baffling his pursuers.

On the same day, Fr. Francis Helan, a very aged Franciscan, was seized at the foot of the altar, in Drogheda, just as he had concluded Mass. While being hurried through the town as a prisoner, the news spread, the women rushed from all sides, stones and missiles were used with great effect, and he was rescued. Fearing, however, that the Catholics might suffer in consequence, he later voluntarily surrendered himself and, being tried, was condemned and flung into a filthy prison. No words could exaggerate the intense loyalty of the people to the clergy during this terrible time, and whenever a priest was arrested, nothing was left undone to secure his liberation. "This," says O'Sullivan, "fills the Protestant agents with rage; and sometimes the Catholic laity, who are known thus to succour their persecuted pastors, are accused of other crimes and brought to the scaffold."

After twenty-seven years, a Parliament met in Dublin Castle on the eighteenth of May 1613, but the refusal of the Catholic members to attend Protestant worship, and their subsequent withdrawal from both Houses, greatly incensed the authorities.

The king, being very angry, summoned an Irish deputation to Whitehall, taunted them with being hostile to himself and his religion, and being "more attached to popery and to Rome." Two of the members, Talbot and Luttrel, were cast into prison and subjected to heavy fines. The temper of James grew worse, and on the last day of May 1614, the dark cloud of his rage burst in an edict that commanded "all archbishops, bishops, Jesuits and seminarists who have derived their authority from Rome, to withdraw themselves from the kingdom of Ireland." The royal constables and other officers were empowered by the same degree to arrest and punish all those who, after that date, should be found in the country.

In the very teeth of this proclamation, however, a provincial synod assembled at Kilkenny on the twenty-second of June under the presidency of Dr. Matthews. All the suffragan sees were at this time vacant, and even the names of the vicars-general present from each diocese have not come down to us. Their first act was to profess their obedience to the Holy See and to accept, with becoming reverence, all that had been ordained by the Council of Trent. A church or chapel seemed at this time to be beyond the horizon of hope. No consecrated place being available in which the Body of the Lord could repose with a light burning before it, as the canons prescribed, the council ordered that two, or at least one particle should be preserved at the priest's residence. This was to be used as Viaticum in case it might not be possible to celebrate Mass without delay.

The council further ordained that only the most becoming localities should be selected for the celebration of the Holy Sacrifice. In addition to this, the greatest care was to be taken so that no dust might mingle with the consecrated elements and no wind blow away the sacred particles. To obviate this, sheets were to be hung over and around the rude altar.

But the most surprising and pathetic canon, and the one that bespoke most the tender solicitude of the bishops for their persecuted flock, was that which empowered laymen, in case of necessity, to carry the Blessed Sacrament in a pyx to the dying. "The recipients, if priests," the canon prescribes, "can administer it to themselves in the ordinary way, but if laymen they are not to touch the Sacred Host with their hands, but may, after an Act of sincere Contrition, reverently lift it into their mouths with the tongue." How many a deathbed must this permission have comforted, and how many a soul must, as a result, have been strengthened for the last long journey by the Bread of Everlasting Life.

In 1615, the government authorities were in hot pursuit of the archbishop of Dublin who was "by name and by person odious to the King." On the thirtieth of August 1616, Chichester was succeeded as deputy by Oliver St. John, who during the next few years proved himself not only a bigot but also a tyrant. On assuming office, O'Sullivan tells us, he is said to have sworn the extirpation, within two years, of all the priests in Ireland. A few months later, he published a proclamation against the regular clergy.[25] He built new prisons and filled them with Catholics. By a rigorous infliction of the Sunday fines, he gathered into the royal treasury six hundred thousand crowns of gold, and when some of the poor Catholics of Meath fled from the collectors to the mountain recesses, they were pursued by armed soldiers and fierce bloodhounds.

During 1617, the pursuit of Dr. Matthews became intensified, stimulated, very probably, by the rich reward of five hundred pounds that was promised to whomsoever should bring to the government the head of the archbishop, dead or alive. During the Eastertide of this year, Dublin was stirred to its center by raids. But though, on the instructions of a spy, certain districts were marked out, guards placed

---

[25] Clergy belonging to a religious order. — Ed. note.

at the corners of the streets, and a house-to-house search made, the archbishop was safe in the custody of a faithful people.

Dr. David Kearney, archbishop of Cashel, writing in this year, assures us that the persecution went on increasing every day on account of the new viceroy, who had promised great things to the king. In 1618, he testified that it raged "with more dreadful violence than ever in past years." Despite this fact, the number of priests increased, and bands of them came with joy from continental institutions where they had been educated to restore the ancient splendor of religion. The religious orders began to raise their heads and flourish once more. The Dominicans were again numerous, and the Franciscans more numerous still. The Jesuits had some very distinguished members, one being brother of the archbishop of Cashel, and another, Fr. Nicholas Nugent, confessor of the Faith in Dublin Castle. The total number of Irish priests, whose names were known to the government at this time, amounted to 1,150.

The Capuchins had come three years previously from Charleville in France and were now working in different parts of the country. Being few and having as yet no fixed residence, they dwelt in the homes of their relatives or in the castles of the nobles and cultivated the portions of the Lord's vineyard that lay nearest at hand. Fr. Stephen (Daly), especially, had endeared himself to all and was held in high esteem by Dr. David Rothe, who this year, as representative of the primate, presided over the Provincial Synod of Armagh and was also appointed bishop of Ossory. This distinguished ecclesiastic writes in most complimentary terms of the zealous Capuchin.

"Father Daly is," he says, "my special friend with whom I willingly communicate in all occurrences, and he with me. His cunctation and moderation, with experience and practice of our country's affairs and knowledge of the dispositions of our natives, gave me great satisfaction."

During the five years of his missionary life, he worked with wonderful zeal and accomplished what might be described as an eucharistic revival that shines, like a ray of sunshine, through the darkness of this troubled time. He restored the little church at Tessauran, King's County, the place of his birth, and writing over twenty years later, Fr. Nicholas (Archbold), his fellow-Capuchin, sums up some of his good deeds in words that fill us with astonishment and admiration. "He caused," he says, "the Blessed Sacrament to be borne to the sick with bells, light, and honest company, and caused the ways for this purpose to be redressed and cleared.... He procured the Angelical Salutation to be thrice tolled in the church wherein he himself was afterwards buried. He brought in and taught the people the use of relics, medals and indulgences. He caused Confessions to be frequented twice a year, sometimes monthly. He kindled each one to particular devotion towards the Saint whose name they did bear. He daily celebrated once, and upon necessity twice, according to our faculties granted from Rome, which authoriseth when need requireth during persecution time to celebrate twice even on ferial days. He made the *Confiteor* in Irish that is now in use among the people of that district or territory."[26]

In the beginning of 1622, Henry Carey, Lord Falkland, came over as lord deputy. On his being sworn into office, Ussher, bishop of Meath, preached from the text of St. Paul to the Romans: "He beareth not the sword in vain." The sermon was really a fanatical harangue urging the new deputy to put the penal statutes into full force against the Irish Catholics. In February of the following year, a proclamation was published against Catholic priests of all kinds, ordering them to quit the kingdom within forty days, and after this, forbidding all persons to hold any converse with them.

[26] Archbold, *Historie of the Irish Capucins*, MS., p. 76.

Things seemed now to have reached a climax, and in writing to Rome in this month and year, Dr. Matthews gives a brief account of the sad condition of the Catholics. Having mentioned the harm done to Catholicism by the Court of Wards which was really meant "to weed out popery," and to pauperize or Protestantize every landowner in Ireland, he assures us that the adherents of the ancient Faith, having been put out of the lowest offices, were not allowed to remain even as peasants on their former lands. The Protestant clergy from England and Scotland were in possession of the property of the Church, and even collected the fees with which the charity of the faithful rewarded the priest for the administration of the Sacraments. Absence from Protestant service was punished by taxes that were cruelly wrung even from the very poorest, and heavy fines were imposed on all those who attended Mass.

At length, in March 1625, in the fifty-ninth year of his age, passed away a monarch who believed fully in what Alexander Pope so aptly calls "The Right Divine of Kings to govern wrong."

Admired neither by English nor Irish, James may, from the standpoint of the latter, be justly described as the recreant son of a martyred queen. Causing between four and five million statute acres of Irish land to be confiscated and allotted to Protestant aliens, he also made many galling additions to the already drastic penal laws against the Catholic religion. But, despite all, the Catholics refused to submit.

Deprived of their chiefs and leaders, robbed of their churches and property, exhausted by famine and pestilence, they still did not count their country as hopelessly crushed, nor give up their cause as entirely lost. A little hope already glimmered on the horizon, and in their hearts they must have experienced real consolation in the thought that not all the cruel legislation of their enemies had effected the slightest diminution in the ardor of their loyalty to the ancient Faith and to the proscribed Mass.

CHAPTER 6
The mass under charles 1

KING JAMES WAS SUCCEEDED by his third and only surviving son, Charles, who, in the first year of his reign, married the daughter of the king of France. The fact that the new queen, Henrietta Marie, was a Catholic favored the belief that Charles I was favorable to the religion she professed. The king, too, was in need of money, and Parliament would afford him no assistance except on what he considered humiliating terms. The Irish Catholics, however, offered to supply an army of five thousand foot and five hundred horse in return for the toleration of their religion and the liberation from fines for not attending spiritual services that they loathed.

The very possibility of such a concession created alarm, and in 1626, James Ussher, the founder of low-churchism in Ireland and now primate, with twelve other bishops, drew up a protest, which they called "The Judgment of divers of the Archbishops and Bishops of Ireland concerning toleration of religion." This document is one of the most amazing compositions in Irish history and truly reflects the mentality

> of such as for their bellies' sake
> Creep, and intrude, and climb into the fold!
> Of other care they little reckoning make,

> Than how to scramble at the shearers' feast,
> And shove away the worthy bidden guest;
> Blind mouths! that scarce themselves know how to hold
> A sheep-hook, or have learned aught else, the least
> That to the faithful herdman's art belongs!

Not a sheephook but a stiletto they held in the present instance, and with it they administered so many savage stabs when they declared "the religion of the Papists to be superstitious and idolatrous, their faith and doctrine erroneous and heretical, their church, in respect of both, apostatical. To give them, therefore, a toleration, or to consent that they may freely exercise their religion and profess their faith and doctrine was a grievous sin." The full text of this sweeping "judgment" was solemnly read in Christ Church on the twenty-third of April 1627, in presence of the lord deputy and his council. This was, of course, meant to inflame the passions of the listeners and to spur them on to vigorous repressive action against any public manifestation of the Catholic religion. In spite, however, of their most frantic efforts, they had to taste the bitter mortification of seeing that, even at their very doors, and before their very eyes, the Catholic religion was forcing itself into publicity, and the hated Mass was reconquering its ancient territory.

One little village, only about three miles from the metropolis, was so distinctly and bitterly Protestant that it was commonly known as "the Irish Geneva." The envenomed vigilance of the inhabitants was so great that for a long time they had succeeded in keeping out the priest, and there remained but one Catholic in the place. From a "report" sent to the Propaganda in 1627, we learn that, a little while before this, a Dublin citizen went to live there and requested Fr. Edward (Bath), O.F.M. Cap., to say Mass in his house. *This was the first time that the Holy Sacrifice had been offered up in Finglas for upwards of fifteen years.* Another Capuchin, Fr. Christopher (Kearney), went there subsequently for several Sundays and, by catechizing and preaching, won back a great number of the Protestants to the public profession of the Faith.

Enraged at this, the dean sought out the viceroy and complained sharply to him of this deplorable state of affairs. But the only consolation he received was the piqued and significant reply: "You see that, even in Dublin itself, not only are they preaching *papistically, but they are celebrating Masses openly.* And, as you say, the same is being done in your own village." This same zealot, on another occasion, accosted Fr. Strong, O.F.M., a very distinguished preacher, and addressed him thus: "You are the man who dares to preach and hear confessions, and celebrate Masses in our village." To this insolent challenge, the intrepid Franciscan replied, "I am not the person who does this, but allow me to tell you that, if asked to do it, I would not shirk my duty."

Poor dean! As he turned away in baffled rage, one can almost hear with pity his heavy sigh, which might naturally be interpreted thus: "If, in the green wood, they do these things, what shall be done in the dry?" If in Dublin, at the very heart of things, the government could not only not impose its will on the Catholic people and compel them to attend the Protestant service but must tolerate the open manifestation of the Catholic Faith and its "superstitious" rites, what progress could the new religion make throughout the rest of the country?

The king's necessities had now become very pressing, and in return for certain concessions known as "Graces," the Catholics promised a voluntary subsidy of £120,000, to be paid in three annual installments for the support of the army in Ireland. The subsidy was the most liberal ever offered to an English sovereign, and the "Graces," which were to be confirmed later by a Parliament convened for that purpose, were fifty-one in number. But of the fifty-one not more than four or five were specially framed for the relief of Catholics, and only one of these promised toleration of their Faith. Yet, though still unconfirmed and inoperative, it suited the purpose of the upholders of Puritanism to propagate the lie that they were chiefly intended to secure a measure of religious liberty for the Catholic "recusants."

At least nine-tenths of the promised subsidies were paid by the Catholics, yet the Protestants, who were to benefit greatly by them, pretended to have a grievance in having to pay anything at all. They contended that the proper way to provide money for the payment of the king's army in Ireland was to put the *law in force and fine Catholics for absenting themselves from Church.* The king did not agree with this, but the Catholics having at length expressed reluctance to pay for what they had not received, it was deemed advisable to allow the persecutions to proceed against them so that they might be frightened into continuing their generous contributions.

In a manuscript[27] written in Dublin in 1630, which is preserved in the British Museum, Fr. Nicholas (Archbold), O.F.M. Cap., who was then resident in Bridge Street, gives us many interesting details of the course of events at this time. After Falkland[28] had gone to England in 1629, he tells us, a "proclamation commanded that none of the Regulars should preach or use public service in the chapels any further. This was observed by the Regulars. Yet, on the sacred night of Christmas, the year immediately going before, Fr. Thomas Babe, Superior of the Franciscans, made some little speech unto the people. News hereof being brought to the State, they holding it for an affront and contempt, caused the first irruption to be made upon the Franciscans' residence."

This residence, which was in Cook Street, Fr. Mooney, O.F.M., describes as "a small house which served them for oratory and

---

[27] Archbold, *Evangellical Fruict of the Seraphicall Franciscan Order*, p. 211.
[28] A reference to Henry Cary, First Viscount Falkland, who was the lord deputy of Ireland from 1622 to 1629. — Ed.note.

convent." Into this house on the following day, about noon, was sent a motley crowd, acting on instructions from the lords justices. Still smarting at the thought of the "little speech" of the Franciscan, these godly men, while at Protestant service in Christ Church, received the additional information that High Mass was being celebrated in the friars' oratory. At once, says Hammon L'Estrange, a contemporary authority,[29] "they sent the Archbishop of Dublin, the Mayor, Sheriffs, and Recorder of the City, with a file of musketeers to apprehend them (the priests engaged in the function), which they did, taking away the crucifixes and paraments of the altar; the soldiers having cut down the image of St. Francis, the priests and friars were delivered into the hands of the pursuivants."

The same incident is described by Fr. Nicholas (Archbold), who gives us some additional vivid particulars. "The Mayor Forster," he says, "with the Protestant Dublinian Bishop and armed soldiers, enter upon the Franciscans *as they were at Mass*, breaking up their doors, pulling down their images and trampling them underfoot. They make violence on the altar. They strip it, and carry away the ornaments. They cast hand upon two young Religious men whom they met bluntly with."

So stunned were the people at this sudden incursion and whole-sale destruction that, he says, "none of the assistants at Mass made any resistance," but he at once proceeds to describe the part played by a certain matron whom he calls "the widow Nugent."

> Not forbearing any longer the spirit of zeal and indignation which mounted up in her heart, transpierced with fire of zeal, like another Mattathias, she raised the cry. She flings herself on the soldiers. The rest of the viragos and maidens join with her. They strike, they shoulder, they catch, they scratch, thump and tread underfoot whomsoever they lay

[29] Quoted by O'Rourke, *The Battle of the Faith in Ireland*, p. 80.

> hands on, so that the Mayor, Bishop, and soldiers were glad
> to hasten out of doors. They were met, as they fled through
> the streets, with a shower of stones, cast upon them by
> women, boys, prentices, and country clowns who that day
> came to the town, not for any such end, but to go to St.
> Stephen's Well by way of pilgrimage, to drink of that water.

Then the Capuchin historian adds, with a delightful simplicity and
quaintness, "It seemeth the Saint would be revenged on them. One
of the soldiers was so tumbled, tossed, conculcated in the mire, that
he hardly escaped death."

Another account tells us that the enraged people succeeded in
rescuing the priests, but reinforcements arrived upon the scene and
protected against further peril Archbishop Bulkeley, who had taken
refuge in a house. On the following day, several arrests were made,
including eight Catholic aldermen who, though in their own homes
at the time, were cast into prison for not having assisted the mayor in
his sacrilegious attack upon those who had met to offer up the Sacrifice of the Body and Blood of Christ. Among the many imprisoned
on this occasion was the widow Nugent, who had taken such a leading part in this strange and stirring drama. In a sense never dreamt of
by the inspired writer, she had proved herself to be "a valiant woman."
She had "put out her hand to strong things," which made her beloved
of the faithful in the Dublin of her day and would entitle her to have
her name inscribed in letters of gold on the honored list of those of
"the devoted female sex" who loved and fought for the Mass in hard
and trying times in Ireland.

News of the High Mass in Cook Street soon reached England,
and though nothing was said of the indecent haste with which the
Protestant archbishop and the Puritan mayor left their own religious service, great indignation was expressed on all sides against
the unruly Catholics and "Seminary Friars" — "the resisters of authority" — who had dared to commit the "grievous sin" of

celebrating Mass in defiance of the law. The English Privy Council at once issued an order in virtue of which fifteen or sixteen Catholic churches were seized for "the King's use," while the College in Back Lane, conducted by the Jesuits, was handed over to Trinity College and converted into a Protestant seminary.

In the work already referred to, Fr. Nicholas describes these events thus:

> At Dublin in Ireland, by commandment of the Justices, Loftus and Boyle, all the Religious houses and chapels are seized upon. On Epiphany Eve, the Mayor, putting this Edict in execution, went accompanied with Aldermen and soldiers, about the City. And first of all he seized upon the Franciscans and Capuchins, nailing up their doors. Then after, the Dominicans, Jesuits, Priests' College, and Carmelites.
>
> The Franciscans' Convent or Residence they caused to be broken and razed down to the ground, at which many of the Protestants themselves were scandalised.

It is quite clear, however, that the sons of the gentle Poverello of Assisi were singled out for this savage outburst of irrational vengeance because of the Mass of the previous St. Stephen's Day and of the virile manner in which the outraged Catholics had met the disgraceful conduct of the sacrilegious intruders.

The Capuchins, after much wandering and many trials, had succeeded six years previously in establishing themselves in Bridge Street, and of this, their first regular residence, or rather of the place of worship it contained, Fr. Nicholas writes, "Wonderful was the concourse of people that frequented this chapel on Sundays and Holydays, not only to hear Father Edward's sermons which struck the hearers with compunction unto the heart, but also unto sacramental confession and receiving the Holy Sacrament, which accordingly was performed to their hearts' desire."[30]

The fervor of the Catholics in Dublin at this time was very remarkable. What has been just now said of their frequentation of the oratory of the Capuchins might, with equal truth, be said of their devotion in connection with the chapels the other religious orders had opened in different parts of the city during the years of comparative peace. But now peace was at an end; the people were denied access to Mass and Communion; and from the shrines that had been prepared with so much love to receive Him, the eucharistic God had to flee for safety to the houses of the poor in the city, or the mansions of the rich in the country.

These, to use the complaining phrase of Loftus, were "linked in friendship and alliance one with the other" and had been systematically used as places of worship since the days of Elizabeth. "Even as late as 1630," says Fr. Myles Ronan,[31] "Launcelot Bulkeley, Protestant Archbishop of Dublin, in his visitation of the diocese, confesses that certain of these houses were recognised as the Mass-houses of certain districts. So that even seventy years after the Act of Uniformity had been passed, the haunts of Catholics for almost public worship were well known."

The confiscation of the public chapels and houses of the regulars that began in Dublin continued in Cork, and soon spread over all the other parts of the country. The storm was thought by some to be the fiercest yet endured, but after about eighteen months or less, it abated, and as Dr. Thomas Fleming, O.F.M., archbishop of Dublin and primate of Ireland, testifies, during the slight toleration that ensued, Mass was said in private houses. In his brief relation to Rome, in October 1632, he also says that each district in the diocese had a

---

[30] Archbold, *Historie of the Irish Capucins*, MS., p. 40.
[31] Ronan, *The Reformation in Ireland*, p. 140.

priest who administered the Sacraments wherever needed and celebrated Mass on Sundays and holy days, unless compelled momentarily by the violence of the persecution to lie concealed.

In the same year, the Capuchins stole back to the street from which they had been banished two years previously, and, says Fr. Barnaby (Barnewall), O.F.M. Cap., "although living in stealth and secrecy, they endeavoured to carry out some form of community life" and to minister to the people by every means in their power. Their former residence had been converted into a college, which was called St. Stephen's Hall. Writing of this on the eleventh of July 1635, an English traveler, Sir William Brereton, says, "We also saw St. Stephen's Hall wherein were disposed about eighteen scholars, who are members of the College (Trinity College) whereunto this College was annexed. This sometimes (till Epiphany Eve 1630) was a cloister for the Capuchins who said Mass and preached in a pretty little chapel or chamber. This was likewise taken from them about that time and now there are prayers in it twice a day."

But prayers twice a day could not bring back the glory of the pretty little chapel. The tinkle of the bell was silent, the rapture of the elevation was gone, and the sanctity of the Mass was no more. No sermons by Fr. Edward now, no sacramental grace flowing from the confessional or the altar, no concourse of people on Sundays and holy days! But, nevertheless, all this was still quietly going on in another house, in the same street, at the very time in which Brereton wrote, for the viceroy, Strafford, was busy with other things.

The slight toleration which he had, for his own ends, extended to the Catholics was one of the charges brought against him during his trial. When English Puritanism, backed by Irish Protestantism, had at length sent him to the scaffold in May 1641, there seemed little hope left for Irish Catholics. Hated by those in authority in England and Scotland, they "found not a generous friend, a pitying foe." With dangers on all sides, they could see nothing awaiting them but destruction. Slowly, therefore, but reluctantly, the conviction was borne in upon them that there was no salvation possible except in recourse to arms.

The lords justices William Parsons and John Borlase had broken with Charles and were in sympathy with the Parliament. All efforts to secure toleration having failed, the twelfth of October was fixed for a simultaneous rising. Within a week, nearly the whole of Ulster was in the hands of the insurgents, and though the plans for the capture of Dublin Castle miscarried, the movement soon spread with enthusiasm over the rest of Ireland. On the eighth of December, the English Parliament answered by passing an act declaring that the Catholic religion should never be tolerated in Ireland, and the commander of the Irish forces was instructed to slay all "rebels and their interests and relievers, by all ways and means he may."

On New Year's Day 1642, there arrived in Dublin a fresh supply of soldiers under the command of Sir Simon Harcourt, a rank Puritan and bitter enemy of Catholics. These men, to quote Fr. Nicholas again, "not abiding the very mention of Mass," began by persecuting the clergy and, proceeding little by little, at last broke into the chapels, without any order from the state, tore down the pictures, overturned the altars, smashed the statues, and trampled underfoot every evidence of religion.

They then turned the houses of God into courts of guard so that the priests and religious were compelled to offer up the Holy Sacrifice by stealth in the residences of private citizens. This, however, was soon discovered by the spying soldiers who often rushed in, arrested them at the very altar, and marched them off to prison. The Capuchins at this time were still living in Bridge Street, occupying the front portion of a large house, which looked out on the street. Only "very privately and rarely" could they say Mass in it now, owing to the fact that the military were billeted on the people around, seven and eight of them being sometimes in the same building. Twice Fr.

Felix (Conroy), O.F.M. Cap., was arrested, after having offered up the Divine Victim secretly, and hurried off to prison, being deprived of his mantle, books, and other belongings, including the silver chalice that he had used at the altar. About five months later in this year occurred an incident in which two of his brethren and several others had the privilege of suffering for the Faith.

The houses of seculars had been raided, convents sacked, churches closed, and priests imprisoned to prevent their ministrations to the people and their celebration of the most Adorable Sacrifice. On the very morning of the feast that is sacred to the Spirit of Peace and Love, the gates of the "Marshallsie"[32] in the city of Dublin were opened, and forth came a devoted little band of two and twenty confessors of the Faith, priests and religious, of whom two were Capuchins, Fr. Nicholas and Br. Simon (Lawless).

Their clothes were poor, but their faces were bright, for in their hearts was a heavenly joy at the thought that they were suffering for Christ. Surrounded by companies of armed soldiers, they were marched through the streets, about them a howling mob of Puritans, among whom were groups of faithful Catholics whose lips were moving in prayer.

The place of embarkment being reached at last, the little procession was brought to a halt. Then, singly, the gallant heroes of the Faith boarded the two vessels that awaited them for shipment to France. The Catholics on shore murmured all the time affectionate blessings and words of sympathy, while the bitter Puritans raised their raucous voices and cried out in derisive tones: "Och, Ochón! The Pope is dead. The Mass is gone." "But," adds the Capuchin historian, "the truth, I hope, shall prove contrary, with an Alleluia, singing: 'The Pope is alive, and the Mass is come home.'"

---

[32]   The name of the prison in Dublin. — Ed. note.

Events, however, were soon to happen that would prove that the pope was still very much alive and that the Mass was indeed coming home once more to temples from which it had long been banished. Already a provincial and national synod had been held. The Catholic bishops of Ulster had met at Kells on the twenty-third of March of this year. Declaring that the war in which their coreligionists were engaged was just, they appealed to their countrymen to take up arms and ordered a three days' fast, a general Communion after Confession, and special prayers that God might crown their efforts with success. With special joy too they made arrangements for the celebration of Mass in the churches and chapels that had been built for the enshrinement of the Blessed Eucharist, but that had been so long in the unjust possession of the Protestants. Pastors might say Mass in these recovered edifices once more, despite the ruinous condition of most of them, but, the pathetic and illuminating sentence runs, "with a portable altar, as had been hitherto the custom when saying Mass on the mountains, in woods, and private houses, pending more settled conditions."

In addition to this, these zealous and patriotic northern prelates summoned the bishops of the whole country to a national synod. This synod came together in Kilkenny on the tenth of May. It adopted the decrees of the meeting just mentioned, asked the laity to fast on each Saturday, and earnestly requested all priests, secular and regular, to celebrate Mass once a week for the triumph of the cause so dear to their hearts. The cause was prospering, churches were won back, and many a tear of joy was shed as they were reconciled and reconsecrated, according to the solemn rite of the liturgy, for the celebration of the eucharistic Sacrifice once more.

Many of the Catholic gentry and nobility also attended the historic and brilliant gathering, which represented the whole Irish Church. Frequent conversations were held between clergy and laity. At length, by common consent, the Catholics banded themselves together in an association that was eventually called the Confederation of Kilkenny.

At the end of July 1643, Fr. Peter Scarampi of the Oratory arrived at Wexford as the special representative of Urban VIII. He did not come empty-handed but brought letters to different prominent persons and "wine from the Royal Pope," in the shape of a generous supply of ammunition, as well as thirty thousand Roman scudi, collected in the Eternal City by Fr. Luke Wadding, O.F.M. Strongly opposing the mooted cessation of hostilities, Scarampi sympathized wholeheartedly with the Catholics and gave fearless expression to the opinion, which he knew well was held in Rome, that they should carry on the war till they had won, not mere toleration but *full liberty* for the public practice of their religion.

Meanwhile, a new pope had ascended the Chair of Peter. Innocent X, from the very beginning of his reign, had evinced the keenest interest in the Irish Church and in the war for the Faith. In testimony of this interest, he decided to send a nuncio of high ecclesiastical rank to encourage the Confederates to continue their patriotic and religious struggle. Accordingly, on the twenty-first of October 1644, there arrived in the Bay of Kenmare John Baptist Rinuccini, prince archbishop of Fermo in Italy, as nuncio extraordinary of the pope to the Confederation of Kilkenny. Armed with the highest ecclesiastical privileges and powers, he brought with him a substantial sum of money and a good supply of arms and ammunition. Among other instructions, Innocent X cautioned him to beware of timid Catholics who would be satisfied with the private celebration of Mass and to insist on the free and unfettered exercise of Catholic worship.

The news of his arrival on the previous day had spread, and people gathered from far and near. Over hills and along the valleys they came to do him homage. He was deeply touched at the sight, and what happened on the following morning, the twenty-second, left an indelible impression on his memory. "For the consolation of an immense concourse of people from the surrounding districts," he had the intense joy of being able to offer up the Holy Sacrifice, not indeed in a splendid cathedral or stately church, but in the reverent sanctuary of a shepherd's hut.

But could his eyes have pierced the haze of the succeeding eleven months, his spirit would have been still more gladdened by the signal victory of Benburb and all that it promised for the Faith. Though the battle was fought on the fifth of June 1646, the news of the victory did not reach the nuncio at Limerick till Saturday, the thirteenth, the thirty-two standards captured from the Scots arriving at the same time. Borne through the streets from the church of St. Francis on the following morning, they were hailed by the frantic excitement of cheering crowds and deposited in St. Mary's to the music of a vibrant *Te Deum*, which filled every part of the sacred edifice.

But all felt that even this glorious canticle of the Church could not satisfy their religious feelings and that nothing but the eucharistic Sacrifice could adequately offer their jubilant thanks to the Lord of Hosts. On the morrow, therefore, in presence of three bishops, one archbishop, and the papal nuncio, the nobility and gentry, the magistrates, the mayor, and an immense congregation, accompanied by all the splendor of liturgical observance, a solemn High Mass was offered up by Msgr. Massari, the dean of Fermo, in the cathedral. Thus was adequate praise rendered to the good God "Who fought among the valiant ones, and overthrew the nations that were assembled against them to destroy the sanctuary." It was the fifteenth of June, the day that had been fixed upon by the Scots for their entry into Kilkenny.

Joy filled the hearts of the Confederates, and perhaps, in this hour of triumph, they saw the dawn of the glory that would accrue to the Most High by the restoration of that official public worship that was the most vital thing for which they had taken up arms, almost six years previously. After Benburb, O'Neill exultantly called his army the Catholic army and gloried in supporting the clergy and the nuncio.

But treachery was again at work, and in the following year when Ormond[33] surrendered Dublin to the Puritans, the most vigorous measures were put in force against the Catholics. They were all commanded to leave the city. To remain even for one night within its walls or in the suburbs was a capital crime. Not only confiscation but also death was decreed against those who received into their houses any priest or Jesuit. To them no shelter was to be granted where they could say Mass, and to all that would give information against the violators of this decree were held out large rewards that amounted to £20 and even more.

This year, 1647, was indeed "a disastrous one for Ireland." While the fury of the Puritans was directed with united aim against anything Catholic, the forces of the Confederation had been divided by the incessant plotting of the false Ormond. Between him and them peace was signed on the seventeenth of January 1649, and on the thirtieth, Charles I was beheaded. The army was triumphant in England; the Confederation was dissolved in Ireland; and the few years of open practice of the old Faith in Catholic quarters had come to an end. With the enforced departure of the nuncio from Galway on the morning of the twenty-fifth of February, all hope of a national union was quenched, and the dark night of spiritual desolation had already cast its shadow on a devoted but bewildered people.

---

[33] James Butler, First Duke of Ormond. — Ed. note.

CHAPTER 7

cromwell and the mass

THE DARKEST AND DIREST hour of the religious history of Ireland was that in which Cromwell set his iron foot on this faithful land. For half a century and more, Irish Catholics had, indeed, endured sufferings that were ever increasing, but the full vial of fanatical hate was not poured out upon them till this inhuman monster, the living incarnation of triumphant Puritanism, landed in Dublin on the fourteenth of August 1649. He stabled his horses in St. Patrick's Cathedral, and shortly afterwards addressing his soldiers, he let them know that the Catholic religion was to be swept away, and they felt that the chief objects of their vengeance should be the churches, the priests, and the Mass.

After a brief rest, he set out for Drogheda. The inhabitants of this town, knowing well what to expect from such fanaticism, nerved themselves for the approaching combat by assisting at Mass in the great church of St. Peter. They closed their gates, indeed, and manned their city walls, but in this hour of awful expectancy, their hearts turned first to the God of Battles, and at the foot of the altar, they implored His blessing on the coming fight.

Once, twice, and a third time, they withstood the furious Puritanical hordes; once, twice, and a third time, they flung back the raging thousands from their walls and refused to lay down arms till they had wrung from the enemy a reluctant promise of quarter. The promise was broken;

the garrison was slaughtered; and the streets ran red with blood. Cromwell gloated over the savage butchery, and writing to Speaker Louthall, he refers to the public Mass that had been celebrated at St. Peter's and then adds with special delectation, "And in this very place near one thousand of them were knocked on the head promiscuously, but two."

As a matter of fact, these two were taken and executed the next day; every Catholic soldier was put to the sword; the slaughter of the inhabitants continued for five days, and the savage Puritan troops spared neither age nor sex. The Earl of Ormond, writing to the secretary of Charles II, declared that "Cromwell had exceeded himself … in breach of faith and bloody inhumanity." Evidently anticipating some reproof from his own masters, this cunning old fox hastened to justify himself, not by saying that these "barbarous wretches" had stubbornly defended their city, but that they had been guilty of something more hateful still — "they had set up the Mass."

Reeking still with the blood of Drogheda, and raging furiously against the Mass, Cromwell sat down before Wexford. The city was betrayed by the wretched Stafford, and the streets and churches were crimsoned with Catholic blood. Flushed with a victory won by treachery, this Puritan scourge now invited all the other cities and towns to surrender. If they but consented to receive Parliamentary garrisons, their property and goods were to be secured to them, and no inquiries were to be made regarding their Faith. Only one thing was asked and sternly demanded — a mere trifle to be sure! — that they should abolish the Mass.

"For," said Cromwell, "*wherever the authority of Parliament extends the Mass shall not be tolerated*." What answers did the Irish Catholics give to this monstrous condition? To their eternal credit be it said they rejected it with scorn, and no Irish city was found willing to purchase the security of its property by the abolition of the Grand Sacrifice of their creed.

In December of this year, the Irish bishops met at Clonmacnoise, and the result of their deliberations was published about the middle of the month. Among other things, they warned the people to expect nothing from Cromwell, reminded them that he had slaughtered all the Catholics at Drogheda and Wexford, and recalled his declaration at New Ross that he would not tolerate the Mass.

In January 1650, from his headquarters at Youghal, he wrote a lengthy reply charged with Puritanical venom against the Catholic religion and bristling with sneers at the bishops. "By what authority," he says, "was the Mass exercised in these places or in any part of the Dominions of England, or Ireland, or the Kingdom of Scotland? You were *intruders* herein. You were open violators of the known laws!... And through the troubles you made, the miseries you brought on this nation ... through the desolations you made in the country, did you recover again the exercise of the Mass? ... *I shall not, where I have power, and the Lord is pleased to bless me, suffer the exercise of the Mass where I can take notice of it.*"

"Of threats he is profuse," says Canon D'Alton,[34] "but he will not interfere with Catholics because of their religion, only he will not allow the Mass, as if he were to say he would not interfere with a man eating but would allow him no food, nor would he prevent him enjoying the sunlight but would take care he should live in a darkened room."

The Mass was, in very truth, the light that shone through the thickening darkness of a fanatical persecution that eclipsed all the terrors through which Ireland had passed since the unhappy dawn of the so-called Reformation. It was the great sacrificial act that brought back to the minds of those who were "accounted as sheep for the slaughter" the cheering recollection of the Sacrifice of Christ for our sins. And Communion was the sacrificial food that gave them superhuman strength "to fight the good fight" even in the very teeth of the threats of an incarnate fiend who had vowed that "*as long as the Lord was pleased to bless him, he would not suffer the exercise of the Mass.*"

In the very tempest of his devilish passion, Cromwell some years later devised an oath that, by act of Parliament, every Irish Catholic

[34] D'Alton, *History of Ireland*, vol. 2, p. 316.

was bound to take. This oath, among other things, denied the Catholic doctrine of transubstantiation, made the Presence of Jesus Christ in the Blessed Sacrament a mere fiction, and the Sacrifice of the Mass a meaningless mummery.

Every effort was made all over the land to compel Catholics to take this horrid Oath of Abjuration. Threats and fines, imprisonment and banishment — these were the weapons employed to force the nation's conscience, to pervert the people's faith. All that refused to take the oath were to lose two-thirds of their goods, and this was to be repeated each time they refused. This, it was thought, would conquer the obstinacy of the gentry, who would be reduced to absolute penury, and of the poor, who might be shipped to the distant Barbados.

But neither threats nor fines, neither imprisonment nor banishment — no, not even death — could overcome the splendid tenacity of the Irish, nor compel them to swear what they knew well was a most blasphemous lie. Faithful Mother Éire[35] sacrificed all her material wealth, but she held fast the pearl of great price given to her by St. Patrick. This she hid within her bosom; she wrapped her cloak around it and pressed it to her heart.

Threatened and tortured like a convicted criminal, struck in the face like her Divine Master, cast upon the ground and trampled underfoot, she still held it fast. From the earth whereon she lay, wounded and bleeding, she looked up into the face of her torturer and declared her eternal defiance. Then, turning her eyes to the Catholic Church and fixing her gaze on the altar, she murmured in deathless love: "Cold in the earth at Thy feet I would rather be Than wed what I love not, or turn one thought from Thee."

The very lifeblood of the nation was ebbing fast. It seemed at last that the end was approaching, but the end was not yet! The hour of deepest gloom became the hour of greatest splendor, and the grave

---

[35] Mother Éire is a personification of Ireland. — Ed. note.

peril to the Faith in the Oath of Abjuration was the signal for a grand exhibition of devotion on the part of the priests.

Forth from their hiding places they came, and went fearlessly from house to house exhorting rich and poor to despise temporal possessions, to think of eternal rewards, and to remember that "the sufferings of this time are not worthy to be compared with the glory to come" (Rom. 8:18). These words cheered the hearts of the people, roused their spirit of faith, and brought out the perfect Christian mentality that actuated them to such a wonderful degree that, instead of murmuring against their hard fate, they were, like the apostles, "rejoicing... to suffer reproach for the name of Jesus" (Acts 5:41). They even declared themselves willing to face every torture rather than subscribe to the impious oath that required them to repudiate the doctrines that had been handed down to them from the days of St. Patrick, and to which their forefathers had clung with every fiber of their being.

Here and there a dramatic incident, like that at Cork, showed the fine temper of their resistance, but the general attitude was expressed in a silent, grim resolve that made all "one heart and one soul" (Acts 4:32). So much indeed was this the case that the courage "of the whole nation in the Catholic Faith," says a contemporary narrative, "shone forth with such splendour that a like instance of such national constancy can nowhere be found in history."

The incident at Cork[36] is one of the most thrilling of all in our checkered history. The city by the Lee had already twice signalized itself by loyalty to the Faith and the Mass, but now it was once more to testify to the ardor of its devotion.

All the Catholics of the surrounding country, above fifteen years of age, were commanded to repair to the city to take the Oath of Abjuration. The appointed day arrived, and from all sides the people came in slowly, thinking many thoughts in their hearts. To show their contempt

---

[36] Moran, *Spicilegium Ossoriense*, vol. 1, pp. 424–27.

for the eucharistic Sacrifice, the heretics were accustomed to hold the assizes in the churches wherein it had been offered up, and, accordingly, on this occasion Christ Church was chosen as the place of meeting.

Within the sanctuary, near the high altar, the magistrates took their seats and gave orders that the vast throng should be arranged in processional order so as to facilitate the work of administering the oath *individually*. In the front rank was a young man whose quick step, as he entered, had attracted attention and whose beaming countenance seemed to betoken willingness to subscribe to whatever was required. To him, therefore, the clerk was instructed to tender the oath first.

Quite contrary to expectation, he asked that it should be translated into Irish, knowing well that only then all those around him could fully understand its contents. His request having been granted, a crier next read it aloud, and one can easily imagine the feelings of that large gathering of men and women when they heard, in a language that enshrined the most sacred aspirations of their souls, such strange phrases as these:

> "I _____, abhor, detest, and abjure the authority of the Pope.... I firmly believe and avow that no reverence is due to the Virgin Mary, or to any other saint in heaven.... I assert that no worship or reverence is due to the Sacrament of the Lord's Supper, or to elements of bread and wine after consecration, by whomsoever that consecration may be made."

As the awful words fell from the lips of the crier, the people were numbed with horror, and when he had finished, just for a few moments which seemed hours, all was silent as the tomb. Then rang out the vibrant voice of the radiant youth, looking towards the sanctuary: "And what is the penalty for those who refuse the oath?" "The loss of two-thirds of their goods," replied one of the magistrates. "Well then," added the young man, smiling, "all that I possess is six pounds. Take four of them; with the two that remain and the blessing of God, my family and myself will subsist. I reject your oath."

The contemptuous energy injected into these last words, the angry face, the blazing eyes, the flinging gesture of the right hand — all were noticed by a poor peasant who stood quite near. Swept away with admiration, he shouted out, "Brave fellow, to reject the oath!" The words were electric. Every heart was kindled, and from rank to rank and mouth to mouth ran the heartening cry "Reject the oath — the impious oath."

The church shook with the imperious order; it echoed loudly on the streets outside, and for half an hour there was no cessation to this glorious din of near six thousand voices. The magistrates were dumb with terror, as if the building had been riven asunder. Then, recovering, they rose in their seats, ordered the assembly to disperse, and everyone of them, under pain of death, to leave the city within an hour. With excited mien and grateful hearts they went forth, poor but free, muttering the fervent prayers: "O God, look down on us! O Mary, Mother of God, intercede for us." And their souls drank deep of the joy distilled from the thought that they had been "to God and Ireland true."

Thus in Christ Church, in the city of Cork, the Faith of Christ was confessed as it had never been confessed before. The story of that day soon spread through the Province of Munster, and afterwards passed into the history of St. Finbarr's city. But it should be lifted from its pages, taught in the schools and from the pulpits, and spread through the length and breadth of the land to glorify God and to quicken our faith.

Against such a spirit all the elaborate plotting of devilish ingenuity was pitted in vain. It seemed as if the whole nation "looking up steadfastly to heaven, saw," like St. Stephen, "the glory of God, and Jesus standing on the right hand of God" (Acts 7:55). In that supernatural light, they viewed every evil of life in its true proportion. The image of the Lord's life and death was impressed more vividly on their souls, and His grace flowed more surely into their hearts.

Filled with His strength that gave assurance of victory, they displayed the dauntless courage of St. Paul and echoed, in their attitude, the grandest interrogation as well as the sublimest affirmation that ever burst forth even from the inspired mind of the great apostle of the Gentiles: "Who then shall separate us from the love of Christ? Shall tribulation? or distress? or famine? or nakedness? or danger? or persecution? or the sword? (As it is written: *For thy sake, we are put to death all the day long. We are accounted as sheep for the slaughter.*) But in all these things we overcome, because of him that hath loved us. For I am sure that neither death, nor life, nor angels, nor principalities, nor powers ... nor height, nor depth, nor any other creature, shall be able to separate us from the love of God which is in Christ Jesus our Lord" (Rom. 8:35–39).

This burning love of God, displayed in unswerving adherence to the Faith and passionate devotion to the Mass, can alone explain the adamantine front presented by the whole Catholic body in this time of bitter suffering. Once more, as often before, it was proved to the whole world that religion is not "the opium of the people" but a tonic that gives them strength to support every torture and face even "death all day long."

They clung to their religion with all the sacrificing love with which a mother clings to her child in the moment of danger. By a miracle of divine grace with human cooperation, their indomitable spirit survived the accumulated malice of inveterate foes and, like a majestic vessel fashioned by the genius of God, rode triumphant on the raging sea of religious persecution.

Instead of abating with the passage of time, persecution continued to grow in vigor, and tyrant after tyrant was sent across from England to crush by force the religious aspirations of the Irish people. In January 1651, came Edmund Ludlow as lieutenant-general of horse, and holding also a civil commission. After the death of Ireton toward the close of the year, he was advanced to the chief place and soon distinguished himself by an act of the most refined cruelty.

Marching one day from Dundalk to Castleblayney, this Cromwellian general, passing a deep cave, discovered that some Irish were concealed therein. His genius was at once employed on the problem of their capture, and eventually he decided that they should be smothered. Fires were immediately lighted, and late in the evening, feeling certain that all were dead, a small party of soldiers entered the mouth of the cave. Suddenly, a pistol shot rang out, and one of them fell wounded. Pulling him after them, the others beat a hasty retreat, thinking of the strange ways in which the dead can speak.

Further consultations were held; all the crevices of the cavern were closed, and on the following morning, in the choice language of Ludlow,[37] "another smother" was made. In the evening, clad in coat of mail and armed to the teeth, some more brave warriors cautiously stole along as if preparing to meet a numerous and desperate foe. Just inside the entrance, they found the only armed man lying dead but did not enjoy the savage gratification of finding the others suffocated. With faces bent over a little brook that ran through the cave, the poor men and women had managed to preserve life, but the entire fifteen were at once massacred by the soldiers.

A crucifix, chalice, and vestments were found, pointing clearly to the fact that one of the devoted little band was a priest at whose Mass the others had fondly hoped to assist. They had expected Calvary and gained Heaven. They left the rough altar and the running brook of the lowly cave to enjoy the vision of "a river of the water of life, clear as crystal, issuing forth from the throne of God and of the Lamb, in the midst of the city" of Him for Whom they had gladly laid down their lives, and Who would be forever their "reward exceedingly great."

In the records of this awful time there are many striking examples showing how the priests were punished, the Mass proscribed, the people subjected to confiscation, imprisonment, banishment, the cutting off of their ears, and sometimes even death for merely harboring an ecclesiastic. Writing from his place of exile on the third

---

[37] Ludlow, *Memoirs*, vol. 1, p. 422, Vevay edition, 1698, quoted by Moran, *Persecutions*, p. 283.

of March 1651, the bishop of Waterford thus depicts the awful calamities that had befallen his chosen flock.

> War and pestilence have laid waste the whole country; our churches and altars are profaned and transformed into stables, or barracks, or hospitals. No longer is the Sacrifice offered up, nor the holy Sacrament administered. The ecclesiastics who were spared by the plague have been sent into banishment, the pestilence swept away five thousand of the citizens and soldiery, and still continues its havoc there.

From a letter of Fr. Anthony (Nugent), O.F.M. Cap., written in June of this year, we learn that no ecclesiastic dared to show himself openly in the city of Waterford, and that neither influence nor reward could procure the smallest toleration. "As for me," he adds, "I pass freely through the city, for I serve, as a gardener, the chief heretic. Sometimes, too, I work in carrying loads, passing as one of the coalporters." The chief heretic was the Puritan governor, Colonel Laurence, in whose household "the dexterous Capuchin," to use Macaulay's[38] phrase, dwelt and made himself useful in every possible way.

So useful, indeed, was he, and so skillful a gardener, that Cook, the chief justice of Munster, would sometimes borrow him for a few days. "Yet all this time," says Cardinal Moran, "Father Nugent was, with imminent risk of his life, visiting and instructing the remnant of the Catholic citizens." Searches for priests and religious were rigorously carried out, and imprisonment, banishment, or death were constantly staring these in the face. In this year also, a priest of the Order of St. Dominic, for celebrating Mass and administering the Sacraments, especially that of Penance, endured a glorious martyrdom, being hanged in the public square of Clonmel.

---

[38] Thomas Babington Macaulay, a nineteenth-century British historian. — Ed. note.

Persecution might seem now at its height, but it was not really so. Some Catholic soldiers still remained in the country, and their presence had a restraining influence on the Puritans. To relieve themselves of this restraint, they gave every facility to the agents of foreign courts to transport the Irish soldiers abroad. "Thousands and thousands every month" were, in consequence, shipped "partly to Spain and partly to Belgium." The troops being at last removed, the full fury of Puritan vengeance was let loose against the ministers of the Mass.

To make its celebration impossible in any part of the country, a decree of banishment was published on the sixth of January 1653. This decree, says Fr. Robert (O'Connell), one of the Capuchin authors of the Rinuccini Memoirs, was "most vigorously carried out, so much so that among the thousands of soldiers at that time scattered throughout Ireland there was scarcely a single one who was not either a spy, or a judge, or some such official of this barbarous persecution." Armed with almost unlimited power and stimulated by the reward of £5 for the head of any ecclesiastic, these inhuman men, already fired with hatred for everything Catholic, determined to ferret out and run down every ecclesiastic who, having "survived famine and pestilence, the sword, fire, and halter," still dared to remain in the wildest portion of his own country. Even to harbor a priest was now punishable with death, and three years later the same penalty was meted out to anyone that did not denounce him at sight.

In spite, however, of all this diabolically conceived legislation, many priests, burning to die for Christ, remained to minister to the spiritual needs of the people. Among those was Fr. John Daton, O.F.M., who, with a Capuchin lay-brother and two Franciscan nuns, was arrested in Kilkenny on the second of August of this year. The crowds that flocked to the house wherein he was concealed, in order to approach the Sacraments and gain the Portiuncula Indulgence, led to his discovery.

Arrested at ten o'clock at night by the Puritan soldiers, he was cast into prison, and on the following morning brought before Axtell, the governor of the city. Interrogated as to the administration of the Sacraments and the celebration of Mass, he courageously avowed all, and proclaimed boldly that no power on earth could make him desist from the performance of his priestly duties. As a consequence, "he was sentenced to be hanged on the second next day, with all the additional torture and indignities usually attendant on death for treason. He spent the interval in the most fervent exercises of penance and prayer, and was led to the scaffold on the 5th of August, 1653. With every manifestation of joy and thanksgiving to God, he went to the place of execution, 'and being hanged and embowelled while yet alive, and quartered,' he received the martyr's crown."

Another great confessor of the Faith was Fr. Fiacre (Tobin), O.F.M. Cap., a native of Kilkenny. After the surrender of this city to Cromwell, he remained within the walls and, by adopting various disguises at different times, was able to go from house to house saying Mass and administering the Sacraments to the suffering people. Trapped at length by a Puritan, who, pretending to be a Catholic, saluted him as Father, he was arrested in the street and hurried before the governor. Interrogated as to the residence in which he had said Mass and the number of priests in the city, he refused to utter a word that would incriminate others. "You will be hanged on to-morrow," savagely shouted the governor. "I am prepared to die," calmly replied the Capuchin.

Flung into prison, he was shipped to France in this year, but returning soon, he continued his priestly ministrations in Ireland till arrested again three years later. After months of cruel confinement and burning fever, he was shipped on board a vessel bound for the distant Barbados. "Sister Death," however, came soon, very softly and sweetly, to liberate this brave soul whose "cause" for beatification is now before Rome, and whom we hope one day to be privileged to honor as a martyr of Christ on the altars of the Church.

cromwell and the mass (continued)

The inhuman scheme of transplantation[39] to the poorest parts of Connacht was now in full swing and was carried out with the utmost cruelty. On the third of July 1654, writing from Antwerp to the bishop of Clonmacnoise, then sojourning in Rome, the Rev. Peter Talbot depicts in vivid colors the deplorable state of the country. We pass over the most harrowing details but cannot refrain from putting on record two instances of remarkable devotion mentioned by the future archbishop of Dublin.

The clergy ordered a general fast on bread and water for three Saturdays, with frequentation of the Sacraments, and while "even the infants only three or four years old" kept the fast, the entire people in addition went to Confession and received Holy Communion. This was indeed wonderful in itself and maddening to the heretics, but something more wonderful and maddening still was yet to happen. Through Colonel Axtell, the very tempting offer was made that any Catholic who renounced "the Mass and Popery" would be exempt from transplantation. But though famine and

---

[39] The Act for the Settlement of Ireland was passed in 1652 by the English Parliament. It was enacted, in part, as retribution for the Irish Rebellion of 1641 and imposed penalties that included land confiscation and forcible relocation. — Ed. note.

death faced them beyond the Shannon, strengthened with the Bread of Life, they spurned the treacherous offer, and not even one proved false to the traditional Faith of their fathers.

Some thousand priests were banished, and all the bishops, except Eugene MacSwiney, the bishop of Kilmore, who was too old and bedridden to perform any ecclesiastical functions. The sixty-four flourishing convents of the Friars Minor and of the Poor Clares were entirely destroyed, and the few survivors of the Franciscans and Capuchins engaged in a variety of humble occupations, and exercised their ministry chiefly at night. Of the Jesuits, seventeen disguised themselves as soldiers, masons, and bakers, or remained in the hills and woods.

But even in such places, they were not always safe and had to be on constant guard against the attacks of more than one enemy. In Gostlelack, a district of Connacht, during the absence of his servant in search of a little food, a poor priest was torn to pieces and almost wholly devoured by wolves. In this same year, 1654, we learn from many sources that the confessors of Christ had to live "in the mountains and forests, and often, too, in the midst of bogs, to escape the cavalry of the heretics."

So close indeed at times was this pursuit, and so strict the watch, that, being surrounded on all sides and quite unable to leave his place of concealment, Fr. John Carolan died of starvation. Another, Fr. Christopher Netterville, S.J., after hiding for a year in a family burial vault, had to flee to a quarry; while yet another found refuge in a deep pit, from which he emerged at intervals to minister to the afflicted people.

At this period, all priests carried with them a sufficient number of consecrated hosts, not only to strengthen themselves with the Blessed Sacrament during the raging persecution, but also to communicate the sick and dying. Yet, in view of the incessant vigilance of the Puritans, it is almost a miracle that any priest survived. They did survive, nevertheless, and priests as well as people still remained who despised every edict and braved every danger for their beloved Mass. In proof of this, let the following incident suffice.

On the morning of January 8, 1655, a priest had stolen to the Castle of Baltrasna, in the County Meath, to offer up the Holy Sacrifice. The military somehow heard of his presence and made a raid on the castle. It was, however, bravely defended by Richard and Thomas Tuite, Edmund and George Barnewall, and William Fitzsimons, who kept the soldiers at bay till the minister of God had escaped. Only then did they lay down arms. All were at once arrested, and their goods being confiscated, the booty was claimed by the soldiers on the ground that the castle had been defended against them "with arms and ammunition by those who maintained a priest in his idolatrous worship of opposition to the State."

The "idolatrous worship" of the priest was the Mass. The Mass was what roused the diabolical hatred of the Puritan wolves, causing them to violate even the most elementary rights of justice wherever a priest was concerned. Of this we have evidence in a trial that took place at Wexford on April 14 of this very year. The Rev. Daniel O'Brien, dean of Ferns, who six years previously figured in a famous Mass scene, Fr. Luke Bergin of the Cistercian Order, and Fr. James Murphy, a secular priest, were brought before a Protestant jury. After close examination, they declared that no crime had been proved against them, but on hearing this, the judge laid down the law that *"no crime could be more heinous than to be a priest."* A verdict of guilty was, accordingly, at once pronounced, the three priests were hanged within the city walls, and buried outside in the ruined enclosure of the Monastery of St. Francis on Easter Saturday of this year.

From a letter written in Galway on the eighteenth of July by Fr. Anthony (Nugent), O.F.M. Cap., to his brother Capuchin, Fr. Chrysostom (Kearney), in Charleville, France, we learn that, despite his many disguises "the better to administer the Sacraments," he was betrayed in Waterford. Providentially making his escape from prison, after many adventures, he reached Galway and was now passing off as a Scotch peddler, hawking about cheap goods for sale. Within two years, he was three times detected by spies, but each time succeeded in eluding them, but was now at his wits' end, not even having the necessaries of life.

He then goes on to tell us that Fr. Bernard, a confrère, discharged the missionary duties in the neighborhood. Yet, he adds:

> I have no doubt he will soon end his life on the gallows, for he exercises his ministry in the most dangerous places, and is eagerly pursued by the heretics. Father Gregory is in the County Cork, but we dare not visit him, the road is so beset with dangers, and so many guards of soldiers are stationed everywhere.... We have here an abundant spiritual harvest, for the leading Catholics of the other three Provinces are transplanted hither to Connacht. A few missionaries still remain despite the havoc made by the persecution.... The gallows is always impending over us; yet we never were in better spirits than in those evil days, although, like Nabuchodonosor, we have to feed with the beasts of the field.

In the very ship that was bearing away the letter from which we take these details, thirty priests were being sent into exile from Galway, eight from Limerick, and others from Cork. He concludes by asking for others to take their place, since, he says, "of necessity this Kingdom must soon be in want of apostolic labourers."[40]

On December 10, 1655, Br. Edward, a Capuchin, arrived in Cork from England and proceeded at once to visit Fr. Michael, whom he found laboring in the De Courcey district around Kinsale. In a letter written in 1656, he says:

---

[40] Moran, *Spicilegium Ossoriense*, vol. 2, pp. 148, 149.

Nothing could be more delightful than to witness the wonderful devotion of the inhabitants of that district. They follow Fr. Michael from place to place, so that they may be able to approach the Sacraments. Consequently, wherever he happens to be celebrating has all the appearance of a great Festival. He celebrates, but only in some hidden place, because if he did so in any house, he might be arrested, and the owner of the house and all those present would be punished.

He usually celebrates *twice* each day, and for greater safety he always does so early in the morning, and even at this early hour, before daybreak, there are always some people present. He also administers the Sacrament of Penance and Holy Communion. He has at all times to undergo very much hardship and suffering, and he himself told me that at times he has only water with which to slake his thirst. Still he enjoys good health, and looks quite sleek and comely even like another Daniel.

After three or four days, the same writer returned to Cork and went to Pilltown, about two miles beyond Youghal, where with great difficulty he found another Capuchin, of whom he writes in the following terms:

I came to the residence of Mr. Thomas Walsh at Pilltown, and found Fr. Gregory living in a cave so narrow and small that a person could not stand erect in it. When I first saw him, I was so touched with pity that I could not restrain my tears. It was early in the morning and he was lying stretched on his poor couch, resting after his missionary labours, he having already celebrated two Masses in the neighbourhood.

I remained with him for two days, during which time I was deeply impressed with the wonderful piety of the people who flocked to him in crowds for the Sacraments. He never remains longer than two days in the same place,

but travels around a district of full twenty miles in circumference that forms his sphere of missionary activities. In
every way he behaves as a truly apostolic man, and for this
reason is more highly esteemed by all men than I could
possibly express to you.

From Youghal, Br. Edward went to Limerick and, about six miles from
the city, found Fr. Anthony (Nugent), who was now in charge of an
area about thirty leagues in circumference. "He is," he writes, "engaged
in missionary work every day, and has erected a number of little cabins
in different localities. He occupies these hermit-like cells, for if he
stayed in any house, he would expose the owner to the danger of being
punished." It is very interesting to note that the first use Fr. Anthony
made of the assistance given him by Br. Edward was to return five
pistoles, which some good friend had paid for his release from prison
the previous year.

Having, after many hardships, reached Dublin, the good brother
went to Swords to see Fr. Stephen of whom he writes thus: "Here he
attends to twenty small villages, discharging most of his duties in the
night time. One would imagine from the large number who receive
Holy Communion *at each of his Masses*, that there was some special
Festival with a plenary Indulgence being celebrated. He preaches at
every Mass. The day I was with him he preached in Irish just after
midnight. He suffers very much from a serious infirmity, but this
does not make him neglect any of his sacred duties."

About two years and a half later, in June 1658, Fr. Bernardine,
O.F.M. Cap., arrived in Dublin to make, as commissary-general, a
visitation of the Irish Mission. Of this he subsequently wrote a very
interesting account from which we take the particulars that follow.
Regarding the Fr. Stephen mentioned in the last paragraph, we
gather that his infirmity had grown much worse "occasioned by his
over much labour, watching, and bad bedding." Since his coming on

the mission, he had never slept on anything but straw, and, continues Fr. Bernardine, "his bed was underground like a grave whereunto he would go only creeping on his belly, and wherein all that he could do was to turn himself. This little hole and the adjoining little cottage made only of twigs and straw, was so privately done and so well compassed that such as came in unto the house could hardly get out the entry unto his cavern."

Passing through County Longford, the writer visited his two sisters, with whom he remained but one night. News of his return after an absence of twenty-nine years having got about, to evade arrest he had to depart suddenly under cover of darkness and in a deluge of rain. Guided by one of his sisters, he had to travel through a deserted place in which the rushes were above his knees, until he reached at last a little cottage in which were a few men crouching over a miserable fire. Worn out with fatigue, he was glad to lie down in his wet clothes "on rushes all water under," the rain still coming through the wretched roof and falling in large drops on the earthen floor.

The following day being Sunday, he prepared to say Mass, thinking the while many things in his heart and regretting that, in some way, he had not made known his coming. But though he felt sure that no one but his sister knew of his journey thither, the news, in some mysterious way, had got about that he was somewhere in the vicinity. At an early hour, the people were astir, and wandering to and fro in small bands, they "searched every little village round about" till at last the good God crowned their noble quest with a fruition that brought solace to their hungering souls.

They found him. Soon there was a great murmur of voices, and some anxious problem was being discussed. Then joy beamed suddenly on every face, a happy solution had been found, and willing hands were speedily at work to satisfy the burning desire of their hearts. The angels must have looked down in rapture, and Our Lord was surely glorified by this holy breaking of the Sabbath. There, in that remote place, in the midst of a bog, with every pulse beating with fervor and every face beaming with gladness, these poor men and women, in the simple and graphic language of the Capuchin, *"being not able to hear Mass in such a little house uncovered the house to hear Mass."*

On his return to Dublin, Fr. Bernardine visited another Capuchin, Fr. Anselm (Ball), who had come on the mission twelve years previously and labored chiefly around Sutton and Howth, "looking after nine or ten villages." Of this devoted knight of Christ many interesting and thrilling things might be related, but a few particulars must now suffice. After the Puritans had expelled most of the clergy from the city of Dublin, he remained behind in disguise and labored so indefatigably in consoling the people and administering the Sacraments "that he often passed two successive days and nights without having an interval for repose." When it was no longer possible to escape the snares of his pursuers, he fled to the country where, however, he seems to have been in constant danger.

Seven times he fell into the hands of his enemies and, in addition to being beaten cruelly, was deprived of books, vestments, and all that he possessed. God, however, watched over him tenderly, and on each occasion, he contrived to escape. Once, having been recognized and assaulted by a solitary horse soldier, he took the matter into his own hands and, in a very striking way, proved himself a good member of the Church Militant. Though half starved, the agile Capuchin unhorsed and disarmed his well-fed opponent, and having made him promise never again to pursue a priest, gallantly restored to him both horse and arms. One hopes that the worsted rider was true to his word, but there were plenty still left to seek out the victor, even in the most secret places.

Writing of him after the twenty years of his missionary career in Ireland had closed, his brother in religion, Fr. Barnabas (Barnewall), gives us the particulars just mentioned and then adds the vivid and affecting words:

> He built himself a little hut of brambles in a rocky district. Thence he went forth at midnight, covered only with rough and tattered garments, and exposed to rain, and wind, and snow, and frost, visiting the surrounding towns, and risking every danger in order to satisfy the ardour of his charity. More than once his hut was discovered by the enemy, and then he was compelled in the depth of night to fly for refuge to the mountains or subterraneous caves, having nothing for his food but a little barley bread and water, which itself was sometimes wanting to him. So great was the devotion of the people in these calamitous times that whatsoever place he marked for the Holy Sacrifice, and no matter how dark or stormy the night, all assembled there.

These few examples justify a prolific living writer who, in a delightful book,[41] uses the following complimentary words when treating of the Cromwellian war on the Mass: "From the records of the Capuchins of the period, a story of unsurpassable heroism might be compiled." This generous tribute might with equal truth be paid to other zealous workers, both secular and regular, and we quote it here because it suggests not only the splendid devotion of the priests but also the wonderful attachment of the people to the Faith as well as their intense loyalty to the Mass.

This loyalty manifested itself not merely at home but also in the distant lands to which Puritan savagery had banished the Irish. When Fr. Fiacre (Tobin), O.F.M. Cap., received his sentence in 1656, he was filled with a deep spiritual joy and thought that at last his prayer, the heartfelt sigh of years, had been heard. He had looked

---

[41] Concannon, *The Blessed Eucharist in Irish History*, p. 357.

forward to ministering to his exiled compatriots, sixty thousand of whom, says a letter written in this year and quoted by Dr. Lingard, had been already shipped to the Barbados and other American Islands. According to the Rinuccini Memoirs also, "whole colonies were transported as slaves" to the Island of St. Christopher, better known as St. Kitts.

Fortunately, in this and several other of the West Indian Islands, besides the English settlements, there were Catholic stations that belonged to the French or Spaniards. From these at different times, but always with the greatest difficulty and by stealth, the poor exiles contrived to obtain some spiritual help, but in the year 1650, a Limerick Jesuit, Fr. John Stritch, landing in St. Kitts, built a chapel at Sandy Point, in the French quarter, not far from the English settlement. The Irish welcomed him as an angel from Heaven, and despite the fact that they exposed themselves to imminent danger of the lash, or even of death, they made their way thither to participate in the rites of their Faith. This was not merely on an odd occasion but day after day, for the zealous priest heard Confessions from dawn till one o'clock in the afternoon, administered Holy Communion, and baptized their children. The beaten and broken Irish exiles, still true to every tenet of the Faith and hungering for the Sacraments and the Mass, responded so generously to his administrations that week after week his congregation grew, until it reached almost three thousand souls.

Fr. Stritch, after three months, went to Montserrat, which was, at that time, entirely subject to the English whose fanaticism was so great that they would on no account allow a priest to land. Disguised, however, as a merchant, he went thither under pretense of buying timber. The commercial appeal was successful, and penetrating into the woods, he disclosed his real character to some of the Irish, who soon spread the news among the rest. In a secluded spot, he celebrated the Holy Sacrifice of the Mass and administered Holy Communion every morning, and then the poor, devoted exiles cut down trees and bore them away for their ghostly benefactor in order to confirm the delusion that he was a dealer in timber.

Meanwhile, however, the watchful Puritans had taken alarm, and returning to St. Kitts, the good Father discovered that attempts were being made to compel the Irish to attend Protestant service, while a close watch was being kept lest any of them might visit the French settlements. The passes in the mountains were guarded by sentinels, but the Irish exiles, despising every obstacle and braving every danger, made their way, under cover of night, through woods and ravines and assisted at Mass. Such heroism filled the French superior with admiration, and in one of his letters, he gives expression to his feelings in the following words: "Among the Irishmen who usually came to Mass I remarked particularly two good old men, who, after making that difficult journey with incredible inconvenience, never failed to be first in our chapel, where they assisted at Mass, and fulfilled all their devotional exercises from the dawn of the day till 10 o'clock with an attention and fervour of spirit which filled me with rapture."

Such wonderful devotion enraged the savage Puritans, who vented their spleen on the poor Irish in ways that almost defy belief. They often beat them cruelly, and there is on record one instance, which was surely no exception, of a poor girl who refused to go to the Protestant Church and who, in consequence, was beaten without mercy and dragged thither by the hair. They even went so far as to seize numbers of them by force, put them on board a vessel, and cast them on a desolate island to die of exposure and starvation. This shipment of our people into slavery went on during the whole of the Puritan regime, and when Fr. Grace visited the Tobacco Islands in 1666, he still found twelve thousand Irish scattered among them. He further adds, in a letter written on the fifth of July 1669, that they were treated with great cruelty, all religious instructions and administration of the Sacraments being sternly interdicted. "Nor," he adds, "can any priest visit them without risking his life."

About the same time there were in the Barbados some eight thousand Irish, who clung to their Faith in spite of all the diabolical arts employed by the heretics to rob them of the one solace that made life bearable. In a small island adjoining St. Kitts were six hundred, whose story, a marvel of daring and endurance, brings back to our minds the truth of the words that once flashed forth from the courageous heart of the apostle of the Gentiles: "This is the victory which overcameth the world: our faith" (1 John 5:4).[42] Following, as it were, an irresistible urge, these poor Irish slaves, cast on a lonely island, again and again braved the fines of their hard and cruel masters. Yea, they braved even the lash, going by stealth to some of the French chapels in order to frequent the Sacraments and to assist at the august Sacrifice of the Mass.

The memory of such extraordinary heroism we should "not willingly let die." It should serve as a goad to our lagging devotion, recalling, as it does, the words used by Melanchthon when dealing with other and older attempts at suppression. "The world," he says, "was so attached to the Mass that apparently nothing could tear it from men's hearts." From Irish hearts it certainly could not be torn, and the instances we have given surely contain, as the seed holds the flower, the germ of a splendid epic on Ireland's imperishable loyalty to the Mass.

---

[42] The author mistakingly attributes this Scripture verse to St. Paul. — Ed. note.

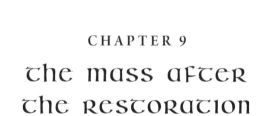

CHAPTER 9

The Mass After
The Restoration

CROMWELL, THE PROTECTOR OF the Commonwealth, died on the twelfth of August 1658, and after the short reign of his son, Richard, Charles II was restored on the twenty-ninth of May 1660 as the undisputed king of England. The Restoration of the monarchy brought high hopes to the Catholics who had fought "not wisely, but too well" for Charles and his father, but these hopes were to be sadly disappointed. Instead of showing gratitude by some generous gesture, one of the first acts of the new monarch was to reinstate the established Church and to give over to its heretical ministers the fine churches that belonged to the Catholics.

What yet more aggravates the injustice of this act is that it was done at a time when the Episcopal Protestants numbered only one hundred thousand, the Nonconformists or Puritans two hundred thousand, and the Catholics some eight hundred thousand strong. Notwithstanding his leaning to Catholicity, the king was too wanting in principle and courage to do the Catholics any justice, and the Cromwellian regime really continued. "The persecution of the Catholic clergy," says Canon Burke,[43] "unless at rare intervals, was

---

[43]   Burke, *Irish Priests in the Penal Times*, p. 1.

carried on almost as actively as before, and it was still hoped to realise the ideal of Pym that not a priest should be left in Ireland."

To destroy the priests and suppress the Mass was still the Puritan method of accomplishing the abolition of Catholicity in Ireland. Ormond and his henchmen aimed at the same end by playing their favorite game of sowing dissension, especially in the ranks of those who should be most solidly united in defense of the Church. The parliamentary union with England was now gone, and the old laws that dealt out death or exile to the priest were no more, but other methods had been devised by the unnatural malevolence of our enemies. They could indeed no longer hang a priest simply because he was a priest, or because he had attempted to say Mass, but they could find a letter that was alleged to have "dropped out of his mass-book," and from it proceed to concoct undeniable evidence of a terrible plot. That was, perhaps, the commonest trick, but there were others by the use of which priests were arrested for "intriguing with the French" or other enemy, for "disturbing the peace," and for the holding of "an unlawful assembly."

With such information the government correspondence of this time is fairly filled. These "intelligences fulfilled their purpose. They cast upon the entire church the shadow of treason. All priests were constructive rebels, and any assembly of the people for Mass was conspiracy." On the twelfth of December 1660, the lords justices wrote to Secretary Nicholas in the following terms: "The popish priests appear here boldly and in large numbers, and though this is more penal in England than in Ireland, yet as these men have always been incendiaries here we think it wise to secure them and prevent them from saying Mass and preaching. We have, therefore, given order to secure them."

It was, however, much easier to give the order than to secure its execution. The priests would not be deterred from saying Mass, and the people would not be frightened from attending. Even when interfered with, they could give a good account of themselves, and there was no evidence of the slave-soul in the manner in which they met their assailants. As a proof of this, we may give two incidents, the first of which is told in a letter written from Belturbet on the nineteenth of October by Captain Sharples.

Having heard of a meeting of the Irish in the parish of Killeven, and not knowing the exact place in which it was to be held, the military force divided. One party consisting of five soldiers discovered the spot where the people were assembled for Mass, and seeing the priest in vestments, they seized him. Some of the congregation at once rushed to his assistance; the arms were wrested from the soldiers who received a sound thrashing, and the priest was borne away in triumph.

Two years later, a certain Wm. Weldon, writing from St. John's, mentions two priests named Fitzgerald and Carroll who daily frequented the place and "lately said Mass, in the middle of the town, several times." On a particular Sunday, the former was found "at his devotion" — evidently saying Mass, which was attended by a congregation of five hundred persons. Being apprehended, the priest was four times rescued by the people, but the soldiers eventually succeeded in making him prisoner.

All these meetings to assist at the Holy Sacrifice were designated unlawful assemblies, and several proclamations were issued to suppress them. One of these, dated the twelfth of November 1662, stated that such assemblies were still held in contempt of his Majesty's authority, and two phrases register the two old hatreds that light up with their lurid fire all Irish history since the Reformation. "Popish Masses," this document avers, are "being said close to Dublin and popish jurisdiction attempted to be introduced." Prompt action is, therefore, called for from all judges, justices of the peace, mayors, and sub-sheriffs so that these meetings may be suppressed and the offenders punished.

In 1669, Ormond, being removed from office, was succeeded in 1670 by Lord Berkeley, during whose vice-royalty there was toleration. In the spring of this year also, Oliver Plunket returned to Ireland as archbishop of Armagh, and being then only forty years of age, the saintly primate took up his work with all the ardor of youth. Already in June, writing to Cardinal Barberini, cardinal protector of the Church in Ireland, he says that he had held two synods and two ordinations, and "in a month and a half administered confirmation to more than ten thousand persons." He adds that he believed there yet remained throughout his province over fifty thousand people to be confirmed.

In this year, too, Dr. John Brenan, being appointed to the See of Waterford and Lismore, which had been vacant for twenty years, was consecrated in Belgium and came at once to his native land. In the following year, he officiated, as assistant, at the consecration of Thady Kehoe, O.P., bishop of Clonfert, and next year held an ordination in his own diocese. From a report sent by him to Propaganda and dated the eighteenth of June 1672, we gather some very interesting facts from which we may infer the extent and nature of the toleration of this time, which was afterwards accepted as a satisfactory concession in the first of the civil articles in the Treaty of Limerick.

"We live in peace," says the bishop, "and the military are to be found only in the garrisons.... Exercise of the sacred ministry is more freely permitted in the country than in the cities, and greater freedom is allowed in Dublin than in the other cities.... All the ancient churches now in the hands of the Protestants are stone buildings. The Catholic oratories are almost all houses of straw."

Then he adds in a sadly illuminating sentence or two: "In none of the oratories is the Blessed Sacrament preserved with a lamp before it, on account of the poverty of the clergy and the danger of irreverence from our adversaries. The Holy oils are preserved in the house of the parish priest."

Though, at the Restoration of the king, most of the banished clergy returned to the diocese, there were still many parishes that had no pastor, and there were no nuns. In the city of Waterford, the bishop appointed an ecclesiastic who acted as parish priest and kept a school attended by fifteen youths. In three other places within the diocese there was a poor school, each with only a few children, but "as a rule," adds the bishop, "all the children have to attend Protestant schools ... where some poison is very often inhaled."

Not only were the Protestants well provided with schools, but their bishop and clergy also enjoyed all the revenue of the cathedral and parochial churches. In addition, "all the abbey property of the kingdom" was held by the Protestant laity, and "this," adds Dr. Brenan, "is the bait they are all eager for." He, on the contrary, had no house of his own, and indeed no income, but was supported solely by some voluntary offerings from the priests and occasional alms from the laity.

In the first year or so of his episcopacy, he had a lodging in Waterford, but the city was no longer the "Little Rome" of Rinuccini's time. Cromwellian bigotry and greed had scattered its Catholic merchant families far and wide, distributing their ships and warehouses among ranting sectaries who hated the pope, the Mass, and every sacred person and thing that Waterford still held dear. "The godly crew of adventurers," says Canon Power,[44] "retained their hold even after the Restoration, and the Catholics cried in vain for their own. On Dr. Brenan's arrival he found the foreign faction or its offspring dominating the city," with the result that he soon had to fly for his life. Retreating to Armagh, he was the guest of the primate, Dr. Plunket, who had been himself compelled to retire for a time to a wretched cottage, a hut "made of straw" on the Fews Mountains.

In a letter dated the twenty-eighth of June 1672, and written from Waterford to the cardinal prefect of the Propaganda, Palutius

[44] Power, *Irish Historical Documents*, no. 3, p. 12 et seq.

Alteri, Dr. Brenan gives us a brief account of a diocesan synod and a visitation of the Diocese of Lismore. The visitation, he tells us, brought incredible delight to the poor Catholics of "the whole territory," and all the more so as in many parts of it no bishop had been seen "for the past forty years." Not a day passed in which he had not to give Confirmation *at least twice*, and his vicar-general, who accompanied him, stated that fifteen thousand persons were confirmed, some of them being sixty years of age. So great indeed was the concourse that at times Mass had to be celebrated and Confirmation administered on the mountains under a broiling sun, this being the hottest season within human memory.

In yet another letter, written from the same city on the sixth of the following September, the indefatigable bishop says, the new viceroy, the Earl of Essex, "is a lover of justice and is respected." He had been appointed in the preceding May, and in view of the fact that he had received general instructions to pursue a less tolerant policy than his predecessor, Lord Berkeley, it is interesting to note what the bishop adds. "He is," he says, "supposed to be favourable to the Catholics. Fr. Howard and Rev. Mr. Patrick have spoken to him more than once, recommending our position to him, and he has always shown a good disposition towards us." In a preceding paragraph of the same letter, he writes, "Here we enjoy great liberty in performing our ecclesiastical functions, excepting on Sundays, for on that day only the Protestants go to church, and while they are at church we are not allowed to hold any assembly, nor to walk through the city. Outside the city this prohibition does not hold; in the city on all other days the functions are carried through without objection."

The Sunday prohibition was enforced by the Protestant magistrate "under pain of imprisonment and other arbitrary penalties." Some of the richer families who could not get to Mass before the Protestant morning service began did not on that account consider themselves dispensed from the Sunday obligation. On the contrary, they took care, whenever at all possible, to have the Holy Sacrifice celebrated in their homes "for themselves and their household."

Accompanying this September letter was a *relatio status*, from which we learn that in the Diocese of Waterford and Lismore there were, at this time, two cathedrals, a hundred churches, and forty chapels. The Cathedral of Waterford, being used for service by the Protestants, was "kept in some repair," but the Cathedral of Lismore was "altogether ruinous as are also the parochial churches and chapels, excepting twenty at most." The Protestants "have never built a single new church, and have not even repaired the old ones that were built and endowed by our Catholic forefathers. Nay, more, when there is question of repairing bells, organs, and similar things in the Cathedral, they compel our Catholics to contribute."

Besides "the fixed revenues," which amounted to £1,750 a year for the Protestant bishop, and to a "large income" for the Protestant ministers, they further insisted on "the casual receipts." This meant that all which should accrue to the parish priest for baptisms, marriages, funerals, and so on, had to "be paid to the Protestant minister, that he might permit the parish priest to perform these functions." The people were very poor, the priests were few, not more than twenty-six, and among these the different parishes were divided, some having to attend to four, others to five, and some even to seven. "One parish," he adds, "will sometimes not have more than ten Catholic families, and at times some parishes are without Mass on Sundays, and I have to apply to one of the Religious to give assistance."

"As a result of the fewness of priests and the number of parishes," continues the *status*, "each pastor has to celebrate two Masses on Sundays, but in two different places, without which half the people could not hear Mass — the distances are so great." Even on weekdays, when there are two deaths in different parishes and a large concourse of people, it is customary for the priest to celebrate two Requiem Masses, but this is done only in the country parts. "Many of the pastors," it also states, "have no Mass-house, and celebrate in the mountains or in the open country, spreading some tent or covering over the altar. This is occasioned not only by the poverty of the pastor, but by the fact that all the land is held by heretics, who will not allow a Mass-house to be built. In other districts of the diocese, where Catholics hold the land in fee or lease, oratories are erected and are, for the most part, commodious and decorous."

This state of things was not peculiar to these dioceses alone but was more or less common to the whole of Ireland. Owing to the edicts of 1673, which banished the regulars from the kingdom, all their residences and chapels were closed, and those who did not leave the country had to suffer much. In 1675, the tempest abated, "and the Religious," says Dr. Brenan, "especially the Franciscans, have, by order of their Superior, begun to live in community, and to open public chapels." At this time, there were, in the united dioceses over which the bishop presided, "ten Franciscans, two Dominicans, two Augustinians, five Jesuits, and one Capuchin."

In 1676, the penal atmosphere had improved so much that his lordship was able to move about with comparative freedom and to hold, at Carrick-on-Suir, a synod that all the clergy, with the exception of three, attended. The decrees of the synod are still extant, and while they witness to the improved condition of things in the Church in Munster, they also bear eloquent testimony to the tender solicitude manifested towards the most adorable Sacrament of the Altar. It was no longer to be borne in any other than a silver vessel, and the sacred vessels that had been formerly committed to the care of the laity, from motives of safety, were to be recovered and restored to their proper churches. For years after, owing to poverty, several of the clergy had to be satisfied with poor missals and pewter chalices, but a little over a decade of years later, Dr. Brenan, in a report to Propaganda, testified that "for the most part they have decent vestments and silver chalices."

In this year also the archbishop had the pleasure of a return visit from the primate, Dr. Plunket, and in 1677, the viceroy, Essex, was recalled. In the same year, Ormond, the wiliest and, perhaps, the bitterest enemy that our country ever knew, was reappointed lord lieutenant. His brother, Richard, it may be interesting to note, was an excellent Catholic. He lived near Carrick-on-Suir, County Tipperary, in the Castle of Kilcash, a place immortalized in Irish poetry by a passionate lament for "an t-aifrean doimhinn," "the august Mass," and "the bells that will ring nevermore." In this castle, which was in the Diocese of Lismore, both Dr. Phelan of Ossory and Dr. Brenan often held ordinations and always found a safe refuge with a warm welcome.

On the fourteenth of October of this year, the latter, made archbishop of Cashel a few months previously, wrote two short letters, one of which deals exclusively with a very distinguished Irish Capuchin, Fr. Robert (Daniel O'Connell), a native of Desmond, whose name is inseparably associated with the Rinuccini Memoirs, now being published.[45] Having studied philosophy at Cork until March 1640, he went to France to complete his course. At Bordeaux University, he signalized himself by proficiency in several subjects, was professed in the Capuchin Novitiate of Charleville in the same country in July 1645, began the study of theology at Paris in 1647, and was ordained there in 1652. In 1661, he was called to Florence to assist another Irish Capuchin, Fr. Richard (Barnaby O'Ferrall), then engaged in the compilation of the vast mass of material that he had extracted from the papers of the papal nuncio, who had died on the thirteenth of December 1653. The work was completed in 1666, and Fr. Robert was "the devoted scribe whose hand penned practically the whole manuscript," which he confided

[45] Edited by Rev. Fr. Stanislaus, O.F.M. Cap.

in its finished state to the Rinuccini family and then returned to his brethren in France.[46]

We do not know exactly when he was able to indulge the ardent longing of his soul by undertaking missionary work in Ireland, but we are certain that he was commissary-general in July 1675 and is, very probably, the "one Capuchin" referred to in Dr. Brenan's report to the secretary of Propaganda on the twentieth of September of this very year. Having now, in October 1677, designated him the superior of the Capuchins in this country, and stated that he had "set out for Rome to take part in the General Chapter of the Order" to be held there in the following year, the archbishop continues, "He is a man of learning and of great zeal, and in the short time that he has been here he has done a great deal of good by his learned sermons, wise discourses, and religious deportment. For this reason I endeavoured as far as I could to keep him here, but without success, as he considered himself obliged to attend the Chapter. I bring these matters before your Excellency that, being acquainted with his merit, you may show him favour and send him back to us. He merits the former and we desire the latter." The desire was never gratified, for Fr. Robert became seriously ill in Rome and died there on the sixteenth of June 1678, with the reputation for sanctity and miracles.

In the same year, on the fourteenth of October, the Council of Ireland met with Ormond at their head, and a proclamation was published commanding "all titular Popish bishops and dignitaries ... all Jesuits and other regular priests" to leave the kingdom before the twentieth of November. After that date, the capture of a bishop was to be rewarded with £10, and that of a regular with £5. Orders were at the same time issued for the suppression and dissolution of all popish societies, convents, seminaries, and schools.

---

[46]   See interesting and informative article "The Rinuccini Memoirs" in *The Capuchin Annual* (1932), pp. 127–40, by Rev. Fr. Stanislaus, O.F.M. Cap.

Though directed principally against the bishops and regulars, the officers commissioned with the execution of these orders persecuted also the secular clergy in the hope of obtaining reward. But on the twenty-sixth of March 1679, a special proclamation was published against the secular priests, and a further one ordered the suppression of "Mass-houses and meetings for Popish services in the cities and suburbs of Dublin, Cork, Limerick, Waterford, Kinsale, Wexford, Athlone, Ross, Galway, Drogheda, Youghal, Clonmel and Kilkenny." These were, of course, the principal towns in Ireland, "in which," it was added, "too many precautions could not be taken." Rewards were also offered for information regarding officers and soldiers who went to Mass.

The persecution was fanned to fury by all sorts of rumors about popish plots, and, says the primate, "police, spies and soldiers are in pursuit of us day and night." In December of this year, Dr. Plunket was arrested in Dublin and flung into a dungeon in the castle where the archbishop of Dublin, Dr. Peter Talbot, was already undergoing untold suffering. Overcome at last by the distressing results of his long confinement, the latter died in December 1680, while the former, the last of a noble band of martyrs, perished on the scaffold at Tyburn on the first of July 1681.

This was the crowning deed of the diabolical hunt, but still it did not satiate the hatred of the Presbyterians, "now the prevailing faction in the three kingdoms," and "the enemies of all monarchy and hierarchy." Still the persecution went on, and three years later, on the thirteenth of July 1684, the archbishop of Cashel wrote that for six years, owing to the violence of the storm, he had not been able to hold even a private visitation, nor for seven years a single ordination.

Charles died a Catholic, attended by a Catholic priest in 1685, and was succeeded by his brother, the Duke of York, as king of England. Being a Catholic, the accession of James II to the throne gave great joy to his coreligionists, especially in Ireland. The position of the Catholics was improved, many churches were restored to the ancient worship, the Mass was once more said publicly throughout the country, religious were seen again in their habits in the streets, and for the first time a Catholic was appointed provost of Trinity College, Dublin.

But in 1687, unfounded rumors of contemplated massacres of the Protestants were rife, and large numbers of them fled to England. In that country, intrigue in reference to the crown had already been at work. It was now quickened, and William of Orange landed there in 1688. In his first proclamation, he promised pardon to all Irishmen who would lay down arms before the tenth of April, but he made it quite clear that he would not grant to the Catholics more than the *private* exercise of their religion.

The so-called battle of the Boyne followed, and the Treaty of Limerick in 1691. The latter promised a free transit to France for the swordsmen and their families, and freedom of religious worship to those who had suffered much for the Old Land and the old Faith. A pretense was made for a while to observe the terms, but ere long the treaty was shamefully broken "like a twist of rotten silk." At Cork in the November of this year, there were not sufficient ships to bear away the twelve thousand men who, with their wives and families, had arrived for embarkation to France. The stern Williamite city had no pity on the broken heroes, shivering wives, and half-famished children. The November blast pierced their bones, and disappointment cut their souls.

The ships were crowded dangerously, and yet a great multitude remained. As the last boats put off, there was a sudden rush into the surf. Some women caught hold of the ropes and would not let go. Dragged out of their depth, they still clung on until, their fingers being cut through, they sank beneath the waves. A wild wail arose from the shore. It was echoed from the ships and died away among the hills. But wailing was in vain. The ships sped on pitilessly, the wind bit cruelly, and the unhappy women and children were left sobbing hopelessly on the lonely quays of Cork.

The first condition of the treaty had been broken, and it only foreshadowed the scandalous breaking of the second. The country seemed now as desolate as one of our old Irish graveyards. All the evidences of Catholic life, churches and monasteries, convents and altars seemed buried in irretrievable ruin. "From the desolated country," says Fr. Philip Hughes[47] in a fine piece of historical writing, "there went forth the flower of its manhood, and its last human hopes. There remained only its faith, its Catholicism, its poor, and its priests. The priests survived. Theirs it was to assist at every stage of the national tragedy. They blessed the hopes and aspirations, they encouraged with prayer and sacraments the captains and their men, they shared in the brief glory of the Catholic revival, and in the hour of defeat they remained to console the remnant that must pay the price — themselves more than all to pay it most heavily."

Despite all the efforts that had been made to exterminate them, in 1698, there were still in Ireland 892 of the secular clergy and 495 of the various religious orders. But after the first of May of this year, anyone found entertaining or concealing a priest was subject to a fine of £20 for the first offense, £40 for the second, and for the third he should be punished with the loss of all real and personal property. A special act was passed banishing all the bishops that could be discovered in any part of the country, and 454 of the regulars were sent into exile. Should they return, no matter for what reason, *they incurred the penalty of treason.*

In spite, however, of beggary and prison, in spite of banishment and death, the line of apostolic succession was never broken, the ingenuity of the ministers of Christ was equal to every emergency, and many of those who left with a groan soon came back with a smile. Many of the regulars passed themselves off as seculars, and even in this year an order was issued commanding that all sheriffs were to keep registers of the popish secular clergy in which even every change of abode should be recorded.

---

[47] Hughes, "Blessed Oliver Plunket," in Sheed, ed., *The Irish Way*, pp. 202–3.

But just as the century was in the throes of its last agony, as late as the thirteenth of September 1699, the lords justices and Council got information that many of the regulars, banished the previous year, were already returning. Penalties for doing so were once more set forth in detail, and the proclamation concluded with a table of rewards for apprehending the daring offenders. Yet no Judas stained his hands with the proffered gold, and seculars and regulars were safe in the keeping of a faithful people to whom they brought their beloved Mass.

CHAPTER 10

mass in the penal times

THE SEVENTEENTH CENTURY DIED, but the birth of the eighteenth brought no hope to the sad heart of Mother Éire. The sword was indeed sheathed, but laws continued to do the work of the sword. These laws came into being at a time when Ireland was regarded as beaten, broken, and crushed forever. The sense of security possessed by the Protestant Ascendancy made them regard the Catholics, in the words of Edmund Burke, as "a conquered people whom the victors delighted to trample upon ... as enemies to God and man, and indeed, as a race of savages who were a disgrace to human nature itself."[48]

"Not in fear," therefore, "were the laws of William and Anne passed," says Canon Burke,[49] "but in vengeance and in the unbridled licence of triumph." They governed "The Penal Times," which lasted a hundred years and more, and of which a Protestant poet has sung in an outburst of sorrow:

> Oh! weep those days — the penal days
>> When Ireland hopelessly complained.
> Oh! weep those days — the penal days
>> When godless persecution reigned.

[48] Letter to Sir H. Langrishe.
[49] Burke, *Irish Priests in the Penal Times*, pp. 111–12.

> They bribed the flock, they bribed the son
> To sell the priest and rob the sire.
> Their dogs were taught alike to run
> Upon the scent of wolf and friar.

The wolf had been hunted from his lair in the woods; the priests and friars had been driven from their cathedrals and churches; and in the opening year of the new century, "a considerable number of the Aldermen and Council" of Waterford wished to "hinder (the Catholics) from the convenient and accustomed exercise of their religion in the city." Three chapels had been already closed since the conflict of the Boyne, and now the bigoted representatives of the triumphant Protestants would expel the poor Catholics of a devoted city from a dingy chapel in a remote corner of a back lane, whose "dirt and nastiness" had been a public nuisance. They could bear the stench of the "dunghill" that the Catholics had cleared away, but they could not allow the fragrance of the Mass.[50]

Even now Catholics were driven from rickety chapels to poor cabins, and from back lanes to wet ditches. In this year also, under date the twenty-seventh of May, there is in the journal of Dr. Downes, Protestant bishop of Cork, regarding the parish of Kilmeen, a short entry. "The Popish priest," it says, "called Daniel Sullivan, lives in another parish. He celebrates Mass generally in a ditch, sheltered with a few bushes and sods, and sometimes in a cabin."

In 1704, however, by a great stretch of toleration, a limited number of priests were allowed to register and to have "Masshouses" — wretched hovels in which to minister to their suffering flocks. But their ministrations were confined to a given district, and outside of that they were forbidden to offer up the Holy Sacrifice or administer the Sacraments. Even with this restricted area they

[50] See a document in Egan's *Waterford*, pp. 519–21.

dared not engage another priest to assist them in the sacred ministry. *No others were to be tolerated on any account whatsoever.*

Should the registered ecclesiastics offend in any forbidden particular, they were subjected to all the penalties enacted against the regulars, and should any of them die, it was penal for any other priest to take his place and discharge his duty. Yet despite all this heartless and diabolical legislation, the spiritual life of the people was strong, their courage wonderful, and their devotion to the Eucharist, which can be proved from contemporary documents, fills us with astonishment and laudable pride.

Writing to the Holy Father in 1706, during an enforced stay of some months off the Irish coast, and particularly in the port of Galway, an Italian priest named John Donatus Mezzafalce, who had been a missionary in China, dilates in glowing terms on the splendid profession of faith made by the people, in the very teeth "even of the officials and heretical ministers."

"This profession of faith," he says,

> is not a matter of mere words, but is most unmistakably proved by their deeds, and particularly by the observance of the precepts of the Church. The aforesaid missionary (himself) has, on several occasions, seen persons of every rank, rich and poor, come on board the ship and observe abstinence when at meals with the heretics, though they were exposed to derision in consequence of doing so....
>
> In order to hear Mass, the celebration of Mass not being tolerated within the city, they go forth, men and women, outside the city walls, and they do this to assist, not only at Mass, but also at Vespers, which, in the absence of the clergy, is sung by seculars.
>
> Even within the city many families have secret chapels in which Mass is celebrated, especially on Christmas night, when the city gates being closed, they cannot go

forth, and thus they run the risk of forfeiting all their goods and property should they be discovered. Nor are they at all afraid of the most bitter laws enacted in the Dublin Parliament against the Catholics.... If such constancy, Most Holy Father, were found in only a few individuals, amid so many hardships, it would be deserving of great praise, but when, as a rule, it holds good in almost all of every class and of each sex, and of the young as well as of the old, it is difficult to restrain one's tears of compassion, and we are forced to recognise how justly Ireland has received the designation of *Insula Sanctorum*.[51]

The penal laws were evidently working too slowly, and notwithstanding every precaution and restriction, in spite even of death in their ranks, the number of officially recognized parochial clergy was still 1,080. The prohibition that no other priest was to replace a deceased registered one was dictated by the hope that, when deprived of pastor, Mass, Communion, and the other Sacraments, the Catholics would soon become indifferent and fall an easy prey to heresy. But as this was not happening, the fury of intolerance grew greater.

Protestantism had at last discovered that the vigor of Catholicism did not depend on an appeal to the senses, and that it was not the stately church, the artistic altar, the beautiful flowers, nor yet the numerous lights that explained the fervor of Irish devotion. These things, at one time, were supposed to explain the fascination of the Catholic religion and the magic of the Mass. But the enemies of our Faith saw now that the harassed Catholics flocked to the mud cabins as they had flocked to the churches, and bent as low before the rough altar as they had done before the work of art.

It was not, therefore, anything merely human but something really divine that caught their eyes and gripped their souls. It was the

---

[51] Moran, *Spicilegium Ossoriense*, vol. 2, pp. 395–97.

Real Presence of Christ in the eucharistic Sacrifice that drew the Irish people and caused them to pour out all the wealth of their hearts in the miserable hovels that He deigned to visit even for a fleeting hour or less.

No inconvenience, however great, and no suffering, however bitter, could drive them to apostasy, coldness, or indifference. In a spirit of baffled hate, therefore, an act was passed in 1709 compelling *all* the priests in the country to take a cunningly devised Oath of Abjuration, under penalty of transportation or of high treason in case of return. But though this most drastic act against priests created consternation at home and abroad, it was met with a brave front by the clergy, and its spirited rejection was made an excuse for the cessation of a wretched toleration.

Even the miserable "Mass-houses" raised by willing hands and loving hearts will now be of no further use. Those draughty shelters to which Protestantism had not contributed even one sod will henceforth be closely watched, and within the four shores of Ireland there will not be found a spot where the Body of Jesus could be laid.

The foxes might still have holes, the birds of the air might still have nests, but the Son of Man should have no place whereon to lay His Head. They hunted Him in the person of the priest, and already their hearts swelled with fiendish delight at the thought that at long last, in their "great" day, the dream of many a fanatic through troubled years was about to be realized. The Irish priesthood, they believed, would soon be an ugly memory of the past, and the "idolatrous" rite of the Mass would never again "pollute" this Irish land.

But, though robbed of their beautiful cathedrals and parish churches, though deprived of their Mass-houses and hovels, the priests and people would not bow the knee to Baal. With the quick instinct of devotion and the grand daring of affection, they once again found places wherein to worship their eucharistic God and King. They went forth to the valleys, the hills and the mountains, to the caves and caverns of this Irish soil and inaugurated a period of imperishable piety, which has given to Irish topography names that would be proudly cherished by any nation beneath the sun, and which we, here in Ireland, should lovingly preserve with the grand and heroic history they so faithfully enshrine.

There is scarcely a large district in Ireland in which cannot be found some Irish name that crystallizes a poignant but glorious story, a great and stirring poem, on the devotion of the Irish people to the Mass. Note, for instance, the following:

> Poll an Aifrinn, (the Mass Hole)
> Páirc an Aifrinn (the Mass Field)
> Clós an Aifrinn, (the Mass Yard)
> Clais an Aifrinn, (the Mass Trench)
> Cnoc an Aifrinn, (the Mass Hill)
> Cor an Aifrinn, (the Rounded Hill of the Mass)
> Árd an Aifrinn, (the Mass Height)
> Mullach an Aifrinn, (the Mass Summit)
> Drom an Aifrinn, (the Mass Ridge)
> Lios an Aifrinn, (the Mass Fort)
> Loch an Aifrinn, (the Mass Lake)
> Lug an Aifrinn, (the Mass Hollow)
> Carraig an Aifrinn, (the Mass Rock)
> Gleann an Aifrinn, (the Mass Glen)

and the exquisite Bórd an Tighearna (the Table of the Lord), which annihilates space and links us up with the distant ages during which this was a much-loved expression of the faithful.

These and other less-known place-names bring back to the mind tragic and burning memories. They remind us of a time when this dear old island of ours was the home of Irish piety and Irish speech — an Irish Ireland in the truest sense of the word, and a veritable Garden of Gethsemane. They recall an age in which the rocky ledge, or the moss-clad stone, the sods of the field, the sand of the pit, or the ridge of the glen served as an altar for the most adorable rite of our Faith.

They revive a perilous and daring period when the priest bravely took his place among "the felons of our Land," when the flock gladly shared his danger, when they sheltered him, as with a mother's love, when they gathered around his altar under the canopy of heaven, and poured their tears and prayers in closest union with the great Victim of Calvary. But sometimes, too, the tears and prayers were suddenly ended. The sentries on the hills had been outwitted, the soldiers leaped from beneath the sheltering rocks — a wild rush, a loud crash, "and down from God's altar go priest and Victim, one in the sacrifice of love; one in the tragedy of death."

The pace of persecution was quickened. The government became more cruelly active; espionage was perfected into a system at home and abroad; and informing against a priest was declared by an Irish Parliament to be an honorable act deserving the nation's gratitude. The degenerate wretches who lent themselves to this ignoble trade were rewarded with £50 for the discovery of a bishop, vicar-general, or other dignitary, and £20 for the capture of any other ecclesiastic, secular or regular. When even this handsome reward, coupled with official eulogy, failed to get together a sufficient number of spies to satisfy the savage hunting spirit of the persecutors, the government stooped to depths that fill us with astonishment. They engaged Jews and disreputable wretches to ferret out and hunt down brave, heroic men whose only crime was a burning desire to bring their eucharistic God to "a religious and enthusiastically affectionate people."

In October 1712, the most notorious priest-hunter, Edward Tyrrell, presented a petition to the castle, complaining of the remissness of the magistrates and extolling his own zeal for the gospel. As a proof of the latter, in the following month, he accompanied the magistrates of Ferbane in a search for priests. They went through a wild tract of country to the house of Mr. John Coghan, "in a most retired place, far distant from the high road." But their strenuous quest was doomed to failure. They found indeed plenty of books, but a friendly warning must have reached the spot before them, and the priests had escaped. For criminal acts, this priest-hunter was himself executed in May 1713.

On more than one occasion, Fr. John Barnewall. P.P., of Ardbraccan, and a near relative of Lord Trimbleston, was almost in the hands of the priest-catchers. In the district that he attended, there were two thatched mud-chapels, but it was only now and then, during the lull in the storm, that these could be used for the celebration of the Holy Sacrifice. While the tempest raged, Mass had to be said on the hills or in some particular hiding place, and during the week, word would be passed round as to where the little flock could meet the shepherd on the following Sunday.

Once, clad in a frieze suit, with blackthorn in hand, he was strolling along the road, and being on his way to say Mass at a place called Allenstown, he had his vestments in a little wallet that he carried across his shoulders. Quite suddenly he came face to face with a well-known priest-hunter who was talking to a Protestant that knew Fr. Barnewall but pretended, from friendly motives, that he was a stranger to him. As the priest was about to pass, his enemy, suspecting the disguise, said, "Good-morning, sir." "Good-morning, kindly," came the quick reply. "My name is Pilot," continued the priest-hunter, "what is yours?" "Your name, (Pilate) sir," retorted the priest, "bodes no good to a Christian." This caused some irritation, but the Protestant quickly interfering, said to the priest-catcher, "Let him pass, let him pass," implying of course, that if it came to blows, the stranger could put up a sturdy fight, and the blackthorn would give a good account of itself. The priest was allowed to pursue his way in peace.

But in the face of all this, the most marvelous things are recorded, and the precautions of the enemy seemed only to arouse the daringly elusive spirit of the confessors of the Faith. The "outlawed" priests, hounded by spies, were now pelted with new enactments against "the further growth of popery." These declared it "lawful for two justices of the peace ... to summons any popish person of the age of sixteen or upwards to appear before such justices at a certain time and place in the warrants to be expressed." He might then be asked "upon oath where or when he heard or was present at the celebration of the popish Mass ... and who celebrated the same and who was present at the celebration thereof." He might even be further interrogated as to "the residence and abode of any popish regular clergyman or any such popish secular priest as aforesaid who may be disguised, concealed or itinerant in the country." Refusal to appear or, having appeared, to answer these questions was punished by twelve months' imprisonment or a fine of £20.

The zeal of the magistrates throughout the land was not, of course, uniform, and wherever any leniency was shown, it was severely censured by the makers of these heartless laws. But on the whole, they were ruthlessly put in force, and the efforts of the magistrates were actively seconded by the Protestant clergy. Friars and priests exercising jurisdiction were constantly "on the run," and the few bishops who were daring enough to remain in the country, being at their wits' end in the face of relentless pursuit, more than once took refuge in the garrets of Dublin.

To evade these new immoral laws and escape the restless vigilance of men who were tempted by the large rewards, the priests resorted to methods of which Dr. Hugh MacMahon gives us a graphic description in a letter to Propaganda.[52] "Some," he says,

> in order to prevent being identified by any in the congregation celebrated Mass with veiled faces. Others again shut themselves into a closet with the Mass server alone, and apertures were made or a small hole

---

[52] Moran, *Spicilegium Ossoriense*, vol. 2, p. 473.

by means of which the people outside could hear the voice of the celebrant but could not recognise it, or at all events could not see him.

And the mercy of God was only manifested the more, for as the persecution increased the fervour of the people increased also. Not uncommonly one would come across men and women with their hands joined in prayer — having got the signal that Mass was begun — and thus they united themselves in spirit with those who, afar off, were praying on bended knees although they could not see the priest. It often happened to myself when saying Mass by night that not a soul was present except the man of the house and his wife — not even the children, for they could not be trusted with the secret.

On the fourth of April 1714, Dr. Francis Burke was consecrated archbishop of Tuam on the Connemara Mountains. The spot is described as "his place of refuge," and the phrase is eloquent of the temper of the times. Indeed it may be interesting to add that *ex loco refugii* (from his place of refuge) is an expression written at the foot of most of the letters of the Irish bishops of the seventeenth and eighteenth centuries.[53]

The following year, at the Lent Assizes, the Grand Jury of the County Galway informed the judges that "Friars were returning to the *neighbourhood* of their old abbey, in great numbers, to Ross near Wexford, to Athenry, and other places" and even — most terrible crime of all! — "*that unregistered priests were actually discovered reading Mass.*"

The next archbishop, Bernard O'Gara, was likewise consecrated amid the hills on May 24, 1724. Some years later, from a return presented to the House of Lords by the Protestant archbishop of Tuam,

---

[53] O'Riordan, *The Mission of St. Patrick*, n. 11, p. 40.

Dr. Vesey, we learn, among other things, that in this archdiocese there are "75 old Mass-houses, 12 friaries, 57 priests, 3 nunneries, and 32 Popish schools wherein he (Dr. Vesey) thinks grammar is taught. There are also several private chapels, *and Masses are often said in private houses.* There, young men are often ordained, and then go into foreign countries to prosecute their studies and come back as missionaries, *whereby the number of priests is greatly increased."* From other dioceses similar reports were made, all testifying to the fury of the persecution and the daring of the priests, despite the number of the priest-hunters. In Elphin, it is reported, "Masses are said in huts"; in Kilmore and Ardagh, "there are 38 huts used as Mass-houses, and many movable altars; in some parishes Mass is said in the fields; there are 21 old and six new Mass-houses"; in Dromore, "there are two old forts here, where Masses are constantly said."

What eloquent testimonies are these brief records, all gathered by enemy hands, of the indestructible loyalty of the Irish people to the Mass! Stripped of all they possessed, they, nevertheless, provided huts and cabins, and when this was not possible, they took to the fields and the forts to assist at the Holy Sacrifice, which brought them again the reality of Calvary and the solace of the Cross. With the priest, and under the forms of bread and wine, they offered once more to His heavenly Father, the Victim that was there slain, and not only comfort but courage flowed into their souls in return. They rose from their knees, as Christ rose from His Agony in the Garden, never to show weakness again, and went forth, breathing the spirit of sacrifice and heroism, to face starvation and persecution for the love of Him Who once bravely said, "Rise: let us go. Behold he is at hand that will betray me" (Matt. 26:46).

It was just about this time, 1725, that Jonathan Swift, already for many years dean of St. Patrick's, Dublin, wrote of Ireland as "now absolutely starving by the means of every oppression that can be inflicted on mankind." While the Catholics were thus impoverished, harassed, and hunted for conscience's sake, the prelates of the established Church, to quote again the language of Swift as rendered by Macaulay,[54] "were gorged with wealth and sunk in indolence, whose chief business was to bow and job at the Castle."

Side by side with this picture, place that given by the Irish Presbyterian John Mitchel. Replying to Mr. Froude, he tells how, despite the storm of persecution that raged from the dawn of the Reformation to the close of the eighteenth century, the Irish Church preserved her unbroken line of bishops and priests. Froude, who always finds it hard to say a good word of Ireland, expressed astonishment that, in the midst of the horrors of oppression, Catholic priests were not only exercising their sacred ministry all over the country but also coming in from Spain, France, and Rome. He knew well that Spenser,[55] long before him, in the reign of Elizabeth, was faced with the same problem and, like him, sought its solution. But while the poet-undertaker marveled, the Protestant historian misrepresented. He could not imagine that they came for other than political motives and would not believe that they faced such dangers without hope of "reward or riches."

Catching up the last words of the English poet, Mitchel[56] gives expression to his admiration in a passage that is one of the finest eulogies ever penned of the splendid devotion and the fearless daring of Irish priests during the ages of watchful and ceaseless persecution. "Reward or riches," he repeats, and then begins to tell of lonely spots in his own part of Ireland where archbishops hid, and of a retired nook, called Ballymascanlon, where once there dwelt for years in an obscure farm house, Primate Bernard MacMahon, a prelate accomplished in all the learning of his time. Assiduous in the government

---

[54]   Macaulay, *Miscellaneous Writings and Speeches*, pop. ed., p. 695.

[55]   *View of the State of Ireland.*

[56]   Mitchel, *Reply to the Falsification of History*, pp. 74, 76.

of his archdiocese, he moved with danger, he says, if not with fear, and often encountered hardships as he traveled by day and night. Then warming to his subject, the poetic prose-writer soars on the wings of eloquence.

"Imagine," he says,

> a priest ordained at Seville or Salamanca, a gentleman of high old name, a man of eloquence and genius, who has sustained disputations in the college halls on questions of literature or theology; imagine him on the quays of Brest treating with the skipper of some vessel to let him work his passage. He wears tarry breeches and a tarpaulin hat, for disguise was generally needful. He flings himself on board, takes his full part in all hard work, scarce feels the cold spray and the fierce tempest; and he knows, too, that the end of it all for him may be a row of sugar canes to hoe under the blazing sun of the Barbados, overlooked by a broad-hatted agent of a Bristol planter, yet he goes eagerly to meet his fate; for he carries in his hand a sacred deposit, bears in his heart a sacred message, and must deliver it or die.
>
> Imagine him then springing ashore and repairing to seek the bishop of the diocese in some cave or behind some hedge, but proceeding with caution by reason of the priest-catchers and their wolf-dogs. But Froude would say, this is the *ideal* priest you have been portraying. *No*, it is the real priest, as he existed and acted at that day, and as he would again in the like emergency. And is there nothing admirable in all this? Is there not something superhuman and sublime? Ah! we Protestants are certainly most enlightened creatures. Mr. Froude says we are the salt of the earth. We stand, each of us, with triumphant conceit upon the sacred and inalienable right of private stupidity, but I should wish to see our excellent Protestantism produce fruit like this.

Mitchel understood, if not quite fully, the mystery of the priest's gallant contempt of danger and of his daring devotion to his people. He bore in his heart a sacred message that he felt he must deliver, it is true, but he felt also in his soul a burning desire that he should effectuate, or perish in the attempt. He desired intensely, not only to speak the words of salvation, but also to lift his hand in absolution, to raise his altar wherever he could, to say Mass for his hunted flock, to dispense to them the Bread of Life that would cheer them in the desert of their poverty, and strengthen them for the last long journey to the heavenly Fatherland.

This desire to say Mass is the real explanation of the mystery that puzzled and baffled so many that were not of the household of the Faith. That this is so may be seen from an incident related of a priest named Donagh Sweeney, a Doctor of the Sorbonne, and one of the type so well described by the Irish Presbyterian writer we have quoted. He had been for some time a registered parish priest of Macroom and, being of a peaceable disposition, was on friendly terms with all the people of the town. At one time at the Cork Assizes, he refused to take the oath, yet was bailed in court by the judges, but on another occasion, he found himself once more in the city and in jail.

Being "old, feeble, and poor," he felt he must die if not released and, accordingly, requested Captain Hedges to obtain permission from the government that he might be allowed out on bail. To gain this favor, he would, however, surrender none of his sacred rights, nor would he make any promises regarding his religious duties. For this reason, and for this reason alone, the captain would make no move in his favor. Writing to the secretary of the Castle, he reveals the whole case and the precise reason of his inactivity in a few words that display the ardent desire of the priest and the cruel bigotry of the Protestant. "If he comes out," says the captain, "he will say Mass, so that I mean not to make any request for him."

Liberty was the reward of this aged "messenger of God" if he would promise not to approach the altar again, but he turned his back on liberty and reached out his hand to death rather than allow his lips to utter words that would bind him not to say Mass for the suffering people.

From these tales of trying times, we now turn gladly to dwell for a moment on a bright eucharistic celebration that, like an oasis in the desert, lifts the heart and refreshes the spirit. The son of a distinguished Irish officer, and the friend of kings while abroad, Fr. Thaddeus O'Rourke was at one time chaplain and domestic secretary to Prince Eugene of Savoy. So highly did the prince esteem him that he presented him with a gold cross, and a ring set in diamonds, on his appointment to the See of Killala. From his arrival in his diocese, he was pursued by priest-hunters, and it was only by adopting various disguises and even changing his name that he was enabled to elude their snares.

When the hunt was not so keen, he sometimes stayed in the house of Denis O'Conor of Balanagare, which was then the meeting place for the persecuted Catholics of the west. In return for the hospitality extended to him, he did his best to cultivate the literary talents of young Charles O'Conor, son of his host, who, subsequently, for half a century, was one of the principal leaders of the Catholics and one of the most distinguished Irish scholars. The learned Franciscan bishop taught him to translate the classics into beautiful English and would not allow him to neglect the study of the Irish language, which, some years previously, another Franciscan had taught him "to read and write grammatically, and to pronounce with the accent and accuracy of the ancients."

At the command of the bishop, he translated the *Miserere* into exquisite Irish, which gave fit expression to the deep feelings of sorrow that filled the heart of the royal psalmist. On the night to which we now wish to call attention, the house of Denis O'Conor, in addition to the members of his own family, was the refuge of "a crowd of reduced gentlemen" and of Carolan, called the last of the Irish bards, "who, with all his faults, was at all times very devout." We can easily imagine what must have been the conversation of such a notable gathering, on that December night of the third decade of the eighteenth century. Among other things, the bishop told them of the Irish rendering of the *Miserere*, and at once all expressed a desire to hear it read.

Then, in a solemn, affecting voice, his lordship began to recite it. Every ear was alert as the numbers flowed along, and Carolan suddenly burst into a flood of tears. In a fit of generous affection for the family that had always befriended him, and in whose midst he had composed many of his most impassioned melodies, he seized his harp, swept its chords, and sang, as if in an inspired strain, the fall of the Milesian race, the hospitality of his host, and his greatness of soul to those who, like all around, were suffering from the religious tyranny of the times.

Night was now advancing, and proximate preparations had to be made for the great event to which so many hearts had been looking forward through all the previous hours, and which could be celebrated only by stealth. Just as twelve o'clock approached, the mitred son of the poor man of Assisi was at the altar, and the Holy Sacrifice of the Mass began. Heads were bowed in reverent prayer, and all were strangely stirred at hearing once more the loved words that ushered in the proscribed rite: *Introibo ad altare Dei.*

Soon a band of players that had been hired for the occasion struck the chords of their instruments, and a flood of melody filled the room. The Divine Mysteries proceeded, accompanied by the harps, and the emotions of those around can be better imagined than described. Every soul was thrilled, every eye was moist, every heart was raised in thanksgiving, as memories of near two thousand years came back illumined with "the brightness of God" and vibrating with the command of the angel: "Fear not; for, behold, I bring you good tidings of great joy" (Luke 2:10).

Thus in County Roscommon, in the kindly house of the O'Conors of Balanagare, with persecution active around them, a small company of faithful souls welcomed the Divine Babe of Bethlehem at midnight Mass on the Christmas Eve of 1726.

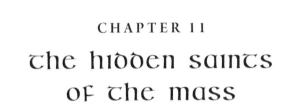

CHAPTER 11

the hidden saints
of the mass

In 1731, THE TOTAL population of Ireland was reckoned at 2,010,221, the Catholics being 1,309,768 and the Protestants 700,453. But "vast numbers of Catholics had fallen victims to famine and pestilence, and others had sought a home on the Continent." In this year, too, despite all the efforts at extermination, there were still in the kingdom 1,445 secular priests and 254 friars. This is stated in the official returns ordered by the House of Lords, which furthermore show that there were in the country at this time 9 nunneries, 549 popish schools, 664 Mass-houses, and 54 private chapels.

These numbers were alarming. Protestant bigotry was once more aroused at the insuppressible piety of the faithful and their unconquerable loyalty to the Mass. Mass-houses were being used wherever possible, new ones built wherever feasible, and Protestant bishops were determining that they must be leagued more closely than ever before with local magistrates to check the flowing tide of Catholic feeling. The report of the Protestant bishops of Cloyne, dated the fourteenth of December of this year, is typical of those from other dioceses and bears witness to the contest that was now being waged between governmental suppression and Catholic devotion.

"There are," says this report, "seventy Mass-houses in the diocese of Cloyne. These Mass-houses are generally mean thatched cabins, many, or most of them, open at one end. Some new Mass-houses have been attempted to be raised about three years ago, particularly at Cloyne and Charleville, within view of the churches of those towns, and where no Mass-houses were before. But the finishing of the same has been hitherto prevented by the care of the respective magistrates of these places."

The number of ecclesiastics still at large was very irritating, and to secure their capture, in addition to the parliamentary rewards already referred to, the grand juries, from time to time, generously offered others. As late as 1743, a proclamation issued by the Privy Council in Dublin offered the sum of £150 for the conviction of a bishop or other dignitary, £50 for that of a priest, and £20 "for the discovery of persons who, being in the possession of a certain amount of property, had nevertheless been guilty of entertaining, concealing, or relieving a priest."

This same year, spurred on very probably by the fat reward, an attempt was made to capture Dr. James O'Gallagher, bishop of Raphoe, who, during a visitation in the parish of Killygarvan, partook of the hospitality of its parish priest. It was soon whispered about that the bishop was in the district, and the priest-catchers were at once upon his track. Getting a hint of this, he spent a rather restless night, and in spite of the kindly remonstrances of his host, in the early hours of the morning took the bridle road to Rathmullen.

Just before sunrise, a troop of military was seen hastening from Milford, and surrounding the house, they began to shout fiercely: "Out with the Popish bishop." Great was their rage when Fr. Hegarty told them that the bishop had gone. Seizing the aged priest, they bound his hands behind his back and carried him off a prisoner. The news quickly spread from cabin to cabin, and from hill to hill echoed the call for help. A crowd soon gathered, and their fierce looks betokened a grim determination to liberate their beloved pastor. Their intention, however, was forestalled by the leader of the soldiers, a local magistrate named Buchanan, who, raising his pistol, shot the priest dead and flung his body on the roadside.

But there were later times when, so to speak, the Master and not His servant was the special object of the fierce pursuit. This may seem an exaggeration, and yet in a certain parish in Queen's County,[57] a tradition has come down on the stream of time telling how, some generations back, the local chapel was on one occasion surrounded and set fire to during the celebration of the Holy Sacrifice. Priest and people were trapped and burned, and buried beneath the ruins. To test the truth of the tradition, during the winter of 1917, the parish priest had the place dug up, and the ghastly reality was established in the discovery of the bones and skulls of a few hundred people, with the chalice that was used at their last Mass. So did they, like so many down the ages, pass away to "the altar on high in sight of the Divine Majesty" in a very baptism of fire and blood, as if to burn into our souls the memory of their indestructible loyalty to the real Sacrifice of the Body and Blood of Christ.

On a Saturday morning of February 1744, an alderman, named Aldrick, went to St. Paul's, Dublin, a little after ten o'clock. Finding a priest, Fr. Nicholas Lynch, in the act of saying Mass, he promptly had him arrested and sent off to prison. Proceeding then to the chapel of the Dominicans, he found two more whom he ordered to be taken to the same destination. Other priests, hearing of what was occurring, changed their residence at once, and thus eluded the grasp of the fanatical alderman. But an old Franciscan, Michael Lynch, very probably on account of infirmity, did not follow their example and, being seized upon before evening, was flung into the same dungeon as the others.

When Lord Viscount Taaffe was sent as ambassador from Vienna to London, he visited his native land. Being in Dublin on a Sunday, he went to Stephen Street Chapel to assist at Mass. To his great

57   O'Riordan, *The Mission of St. Patrick*, p. 26.

disappointment and disgust, he found the doors firmly fastened so that no one could enter. The doors of all the other chapels being nailed up in the same way by order of the government, he wrote at once to King George II complaining of these vexatious doings.

But even in spite of this oppressive and almost incredible legislation, the people were still loyal to the Mass. Retiring to stables in back lanes and to the garrets of ruinous houses, they gathered round the priest to assist at that oblation that is "a tremendously real experience, the experience of the reality of Golgotha." Often, too, as they assisted at the mystic death of Christ on the altar, real death brought them swiftly to His glorified presence in Heaven.

On a Sunday morning of the year 1745, a number of people collected to assist at Mass in an upper story of one of the narrow lanes of Dublin. The celebrant was Fr. Fitzgerald, a native of Meath, and just as he had given the last blessing and turned to read the Gospel of St. John, the rickety old house collapsed. The priest and nine others were killed on the spot, while several died subsequently of their injuries. Public attention was aroused, and soon afterwards the viceroy and Privy Council issued an order permitting *chapels to be opened in the city in retired places* — a tardy concession ungraciously given.

In 1747, the official report of the returns to which we have recently referred was published in London. In the preface, hope is expressed that the charter schools and "the due execution of the laws against the Popish clergy will, in the next age, root out that pestilent, restless, and idolatrous religion." The execution of the laws went on, but the people braved them, and a book published in Dublin in 1748 testifies not only to the fact that Mass was sometimes said in the open at this period but that the people assisted at it in a very reverent manner.

"The poorer sort of Irish natives," say the writers, "are mostly Roman Catholics, who make no scruple to assemble in the open fields. As we passed yesterday in a bye-road, we saw a priest under a tree, with a large assembly about him, celebrating Mass in his proper habit; and, though at a great distance from us, we heard him distinctly. These sort of people, my Lord, seem to be very solemn and sincere in their devotion."[58]

From letters of the internuncio of the Holy See in Brussels, addressed to the Propaganda in Rome in 1756, we learn an incident that is greatly to the credit of the Catholics of Cork. On the eleventh of May, the magistrates of this city ordered all the chapels and oratories to be closed. To ensure that Mass would not be said therein, they not only seized the keys but also published a proclamation prohibiting any meeting for divine worship. On learning this, the blood of the Catholics was stirred, and, carried away by righteous indignation, they rushed into the streets, seized whatever weapons were at hand, and presented a bold front to the Protestants.

These also, sure of magisterial backing, mustered their forces and a pitched battle was fought. Though no one was killed, several were wounded on both sides, and a parish priest was arrested. The Catholics, however, carried the day and won admission to their poor but beloved churches. Prudence, says the proverb, is the better part of valor, and, so far as we know, there was no further interference with places where the faithful met for the purposes of prayer. Cork had once more proved that it was wholeheartedly devoted to the Faith and to its highest expression, the Mass.

Events like these helped to convince the authorities that though patient, the Catholics were not yet slaves and, when provoked beyond endurance by fanatical injustice, could show themselves sturdy members of the Church Militant. How miserable the places of Catholic worship were even sixteen years later may be judged from the account left us by Dean Cogan[59] of the condition of things in what was then the "cathedral town" of Navan.

58 A Tour through Ireland, by Two Gentlemen, p. 163.
59 Cogan, Diocese of Meath, Ancient and Modern, vol. 1, pp. 232–33.

"About the year 1772," he writes,

> the mud-wall thatched chapel at Leighsbrook crumbled
> and fell on Christmas Night, and on the following
> morning the parishioners found themselves without a
> place of worship. For many months after this the Holy
> Sacrifice was offered up in a sentry-box, which was pro-
> cured from the cavalry barracks; and under this tempo-
> rary shelter the priest officiated, while the people knelt
> on the bare ground, with no roof but the canopy of
> Heaven. A mud-wall thatched house was next erected
> on a portion of the site occupied by the present Catholic
> Church of Navan.
>
> The neighbouring farmers used this during the week
> as a barn for threshing corn, and on Saturday evenings the
> little boys attended to sweep the floor and make prepara-
> tions for the following morning. Two barrels were then
> procured and placed in a corner of the house, the door
> was taken off the hinges and placed on the barrels, and
> here the Holy Sacrifice was offered. This was the altar of
> Navan for eight or nine years.

Four years later, in 1776, "the next age" that had been so hopefully
looked forward to for the complete uprooting of our "idolatrous religion" had come and still saw that religion very deep in the soil. Persecuted Catholicism with its thatched houses and sentry-boxes, its
doors and barrels, was more than holding its own against pampered
Protestantism, with its stolen churches and cathedrals. The official
census showed that the adherents of the latter were 751,169, but it
showed also that the followers of the former yet numbered 1,407,315.

It was not till the beginning of the second half of the eighteenth
century that Catholics began to get a footing in the poorer quarters of
the hitherto exclusively Protestant town of Bandon. But before the year
1780, they formed quite a considerable portion of the population and
used to attend Mass in a small wretched building covered with straw

several miles to the west of the town. Later, an addition was made to the eastern side, but the priest was unable to roof it, and when the wind blew from that direction, the people were exposed to its biting effects. After some time, another church was erected at Round Hill, and in 1796, another arose at Gallows' Hill in the town itself, but this was turned into a horse-barrack in 1798. Today, however, Bandon glories in a beautiful parochial church, and the Catholics are in the majority.

In the same year at Tullow, County Carlow, the military stabled their horses in the Catholic church, which at that time served as the cathedral of the diocese. After that, the bishop, Dr. Delaney, would not allow the Adorable Sacrifice to be celebrated within its walls but set to work to build a temple in some sense worthy of the Sacred Mysteries.

During its erection, Mass was offered up on Sundays in a room on the upper floor of the house in which the bishop resided, about a mile outside the town. The windows of the room were flung open, the people gathered on the green sward outside, and followed the priest at the altar within.

Until well into the nineteenth century in the parish of Kilkeel, Mass was said in the open at a place called the Mass Fort, but in the year 1811, a small chapel was begun on this spot hallowed by so many religious associations, and today the place is marked by a splendid parochial church. As late as 1823, there were in the parish of Cabinteely, County Dublin, two old thatched chapels, one at Sandyford, ready to yield at every blast, and another at Newtown on the mountain side. In the former district, there stood also the walls of a church partly built but roofless, lying quite exposed, without wall or fence.

After a tour in Ireland, the illustrious Count de Montalembert published in Paris, in the year 1829, some very interesting letters in which he describes what he had seen and felt in this country. "Often on Sunday," he says,[60] "when entering an Irish town, I have seen the

---

[60] Quoted by Moran, *Catholics of Ireland under the Penal Laws*, p. 87.

streets encumbered with kneeling figures of labouring men in all directions, turning their looks always towards some low doorway, some obscure lane which led to the Catholic chapel, built behind the houses in those times of persecution, when the exercise of that worship was treason. The immense crowd which endeavoured to force an entrance into the narrow and hidden interior prevented the approach of two-thirds of the Faithful, but they knew that Mass was being said, and they knelt in all the surrounding streets joining themselves in spirit to the priest of the Most High. Very often I have mixed with them, and enjoyed their looks of astonishment when they saw a stranger, a man not poor like themselves, taking the holy water with them and bowing before the altar."

Often, too, the writer tells us, he looked down, from the gallery reserved for the women, on the nave of the Catholic chapel as the priest preached to the people during Mass. "This part of the Church," he says,

> was given up to the men. There were no seats, and the population crowded into it in floods, each tide rising higher until the first comers were pushed forward against the altar-rails, and so packed that they could not move a limb. All that could be seen of them was a moving mass of dark-haired heads, so close together that one could have walked across them without danger.
>
> From moment to moment this mass moved and wavered. Long groans and deep sighs became audible; some dried their eyes; some beat their breasts; every gesture of the preacher was understood on the instant, and the impression produced was not concealed. A cry of love or of grief answered each of his entreaties, each of his reproaches. The spectator saw that it was a father speaking to his children, and that the children loved their father.

In another portion of the same letter, he describes what he witnessed in a country district about six miles from the city of Cork. "I shall never forget," he says,[61]

> the first Mass which I heard in a country chapel. I rode to the foot of a hill, the lower part of which was clothed with a thick plantation of oak and fir, and alighted from my horse to ascend it. I had taken only a few steps on my way when my attention was attracted by the appearance of a man who knelt at the foot of one of the firs. Several others became visible in succession in the same attitude; and the higher I ascended the larger became the numbers of these kneeling peasants. At length, on reaching the top of the hill, I saw a cruciform building badly built of stone, without cement, and covered by thatch. Around it knelt a crowd of robust and vigorous men, all uncovered, though the rain fell in torrents and the mud quivered beneath them. Profound silence reigned everywhere. It was the Catholic chapel of Blarney (at Waterloo) and the priest was saying Mass.
>
> I reached the door at the moment of the Elevation, and all this pious assembly had prostrated themselves with their faces on the earth. I made an effort to penetrate under the roof of the chapel thus overflowed by worshippers. There were no seats, no decorations, not even a pavement; the floor was of earth, damp and stony, the roof dilapidated, and tallow candles burned on the altar in place of tapers. I heard the priest announce in Irish, the language of the Catholic people, that on such a day he would go, in order to save his parishioners the trouble of a long journey, to a certain "cabin," which should for the moment be turned into the House of God — there to administer the Sacraments and receive the humble offerings with which his flock supported him.

[61] Ibid., p. 86.

When the Holy Sacrifice was ended, the priest mounted his horse and rode away. Then each worshipper rose from his knees and went slowly homeward; some of them, wandering harvestmen carrying their reaping hooks, turned their steps towards the nearest cottage to ask the hospitality to which they were considered to have a right; others, with their wives riding behind them *en croupe*, went off to their distant homes. Many remained for a much longer time in prayer, *kneeling in the mud in that silent enclosure* chosen by the poor and faithful people in the time of ancient persecutions.

Even five years after Catholic emancipation had been granted, things were in a very sad and deplorable condition in the west of Ireland, as is evidenced by the following fact. At a public meeting of the Catholics of the diocese of Killala, held on January 8, 1834, a petition to the House of Commons was adopted, setting forth some things that would seem incredible at this date were they not enunciated clearly by the voice of authentic history. The petition testifies "that the parishes in this diocese have long been deprived of Catholic churches; the consequence is that a numerous population, destitute of every other source of instruction, are obliged to absent themselves from religious worship, or to attend it under all the inclemency of the most rigorous seasons; *that in this diocese alone upwards of 30,000 souls are obliged on every Sunday to hear Mass under the canopy of heaven.*"

Just about this time, three years before the death of William IV, Lord Grey's government proposed to reduce the number of Irish Protestant bishoprics, and some strange arguments were used against that measure. It was admitted that the number of bishops was greater than the number of persons in the established Church required, but it was asserted that the latter number would not be stationary. The hierarchy, therefore, it was said, should be constituted rather "with a view to the millions of converts who would soon require the care of Protestant pastors." Much oratory was expended on "the expansive force of Protestantism," and while thousands were spent on an excessive supply of parsons, not one penny would be granted for the erection of shelters where thirty thousand Catholics might fulfill their obligation of assisting at Mass on Sundays.

The expansion was not showing itself, nor were the converts appearing. The "No Popery" cry was raised once more. It soon became a great howl, and afterwards swelled to a storm. The faction that began it rose to power, and power begot intolerance. One of its leading members evoked loud cheers by declaiming against the minions of popery, another designated six millions of Irish Catholics as aliens, while a third declared his conviction that a time was at hand when Protestants of every persuasion would find it necessary to combine against the encroachment of Romanism. The monster meetings of 1843 meanwhile grew formidable, the relations with America became strained, and for these reasons, but not from equity or charity, the public opinion of Ireland was consulted, and the religion of Catholics was respected. The prophesied time never dawned, and the grand combine never materialized.

On the night of the twenty-third of April 1845, speaking in the House of Commons, Macaulay[62] declared "the Established Church of Ireland a bad institution," and "of all the institutions now existing in the civilised world ... the most absurd." Then, waxing eloquent, he poured out his soul in a fine passage that boldly proclaimed the failure of Protestantism and the triumph of Catholicism.

Surveying the course of things from 1560 to 1845, he said:

> Two hundred and eighty five years has this Church been at work. What could have been done for it in the way of

[62] Macaulay, *Miscellaneous Writings and Speeches*, p. 689.

authority, privileges, endowments, which has not been done? Did any other set of bishops and priests in the world ever receive so much for doing so little? Nay, did any other set of bishops and priests in the world ever receive half as much for doing twice as much? And what have we to show for all this lavish expenditure? What but the most zealous Roman Catholic population on the face of the earth? Where you were one hundred years ago, where you were two hundred years ago, there you are still, not victorious over the domain of the old faith, but painfully and with dubious success defending your own English Pale.... On the great solid mass of the Roman Catholic population you have made no impression whatever. There they are, as they were ages ago, ten to one against the members of your Established Church.[63]

This English orator then goes on to say that "the quality as well as the quantity of Irish Romanism" deserves to be considered. "Is there," he asks,[64] "any other country inhabited by a mixed population of Catholics and Protestants, any other country in which Protestant doctrines have long been freely promulgated from the press and from the pulpit, where the Roman Catholic spirit is so strong as in Ireland? I believe not. The Belgians are generally considered as very stubborn and zealous Roman Catholics. But I do not believe that either in stubbornness or in zeal they equal the Irish. And this is the fruit of three centuries of Protestant archbishops, bishops, archdeacons, deans, and rectors."

Not all this mighty host could shake the faith of the Irish people or rob them of their loyalty to the Mass. From mountain caves they advanced to wooden boxes, from wooden boxes to new chapels, and from new chapels to more decent buildings. With one of these is associated the memory of a terrible disaster that, occurring toward the

[63] Ibid., p. 693.
[64] Ibid., p. 694.

close of the century under consideration, is remembered by many thousands still living. It touched the heart of the whole Irish race at the time, and recalls a period when Ireland might be justly described as the Niobe of the Nations.

It was in the County Donegal, in the parish of Gweedore, in a spot well-known to the writer. Many rocks have been blasted there since then, the course of the stream has been changed, and a fine approach to the church has been made, but the main features of the landscape are still the same, and wild romantic beauty still haunts this hallowed ground. No wonder that the place has been always dear to the hearts of the faithful, because it was here in this narrow glen and sheltered seclusion that, ever since the beginning of the Penal Times, the poor persecuted Catholics of the surrounding districts met in constant danger and yet in fearless love to assist at the Adorable Sacrifice.

Sentries were posted on the cliffs above, and below on the rocks, a ledge, still pointed out with reverent pride, served as an altar. The sentries were dispensed with when the Penal Laws had somewhat relaxed, and on the natural altar was fixed a wooden box that protected the priest during the celebration of Mass. At a later period, the box was replaced by a hut, open at the end and facing down the stream. This, however, was only large enough to enclose the altar, the celebrant, and the server, while in summer and winter the people had still to meet without shelter.

At last, over ninety years ago, it was resolved to build something permanent, and as no landlord of the neighborhood would even then give a site for the humblest place of Catholic worship, the people were obliged to use this sanctified space that prescription entitled them to claim as their own. Accordingly, they erected a modest structure, which they called the "new chapel," spanning the bed of a mountain torrent that often roared and foamed beneath on its frantic rush to the sea.

This continued to be used as the parochial church till about Easter 1854, when it was accidentally burned. In a comparatively short time, thanks to the fervor and generosity of God's poor, there arose on the same site a "roomy and well-built edifice," which was consecrated on the fourth of March 1856 by the Most Rev. Dr. Mac-Gettigan, who as a young boy, perched on the summit of a high rock, often acted as watch-dog on the priest-hunters, and later as an acolyte, holding a small candle during the Holy Sacrifice of the Mass.

It was this spacious house of God that witnessed the sad and tragic scene that occurred on Sunday, the fifteenth of August 1880. A terrific thunderstorm broke, and sweeping down the Dunlewy valley, swelled the Meenanillar stream, which, reinforced by many rivulets, precipitated itself into the church grounds and the sacred edifice during the celebration of the Holy Sacrifice of the Mass. In a few minutes, the flood rose to the height of seven or eight feet, but, notwithstanding the panic, the young men behaved bravely, handing up the children to the ready helpers on the galleries and placing poor decrepit old people standing on the pews.[65]

To this day, the survivors shudder at the very remembrance of the harrowing scene and the loss of five precious lives. But in the wise designs of God, this terrible disaster, which wrung the hearts of a devoted people, accomplished its own purpose. It "served," says Cardinal Moran, "to fix the attention of the civilised world on the fact that *even in the last quarter of the nineteenth century, there were districts in Ireland where a site would not be granted for a Catholic church,* and where it was only on the hills and in the ravines that the Faithful could kneel around the altar of God, and worship in the faith of their fathers."

These are memories that should be written, in letters of gold, on the tablets of Irish Catholic hearts, and should be broadcast far and wide, especially among the young. Memories such as these must sternly rebuke

---

[65] Maguire, *History of the Diocese of Raphoe*, vol. 2, pp. 263, 264.

our coldness. They should certainly warm our devotion and, with God's grace and our own cooperation, make us resolve to cleave to the Mass in the sunshine of the present, as our forefathers did in the storms of the past. They tell us of the hidden saints of the Mass, the unknown martyrs of our race, whose loyalty to the Holy Sacrifice was like a divine goad that urged them on to the altar even when age had crippled their limbs, when hunger had exhausted their vitality, and the poor body was so weak that it could scarcely testify to the presence of the flickering spirit of life.

In the light of the following fact, who could be so traitorously cold as to miss Mass on days of obligation, or who could be so criminally indifferent as to say that a Mass more or less is of no consequence? Standing in the pulpit of St. Raymond's Church, Westchester, New York, on the evening of All Saints 1872, Fr. Tom Burke, O.P., moved his vast congregation to tears of sorrow, love, and pride by a heroic story of his native land.

"There lived," he said,

> on the western shores of Ireland, a few miles from my native town of Galway, a good woman who was accustomed every Sunday of her life to be present at the Mass, and on the first Sunday of every month to receive Holy Communion. The Famine came. She was then an old woman. Her sons had gone away to look for work here and there with a promise that they would come to her and keep her in life if they could. Her daughters had emigrated, and she was left alone in the world with her youngest child, a boy of twelve or fourteen years of age. They lived together, the old woman and the boy, and, when the distress came upon the country, to such a degree that all were dying, the boy cried for food, and the old woman had nothing to give him.
>
> Wasting away under her eyes, at length one day he laid his head upon her bosom, and, uttering one dreadful cry, died. She was so weakened by hunger that she was not able

to go out of the house to the neighbours to get them to assist in burying him. For two days he lay dead upon the floor; and she, dying — dying with a broken heart, dying with no one to put a cup of water to her lips — dying of hunger and thirst — she lay for those two days and nights beside the dead. On the third morning, which was Sunday, she heard the chapel-bell ringing for Mass. When she heard it, on her hands and feet she crawled out of the house, and tried to take herself to the chapel about a mile away.

Three times she fell on the road. Those who were stricken nearly as badly as she was, as they passed, lifted her up, laid her against the hedge, and gave her a drink of water from the running stream. She fell again and again. At length she crawled, crawled till she came to a point on the road where she could see the chapel door open. *The priest was on the altar saying Mass.* When she caught sight of him, lifting up her dying hands and eyes to God, she cried: "Eternal praise to the Blessed Virgin's Son!" — and fell back a corpse.[66]

This is one of the most pathetic and eloquent stories in all Irish history, a story of the last days and of the last act in the life of one of the forgotten saints of the Mass. It recalls the past, appeals to the present, and points the way to the future. It lives, and throbs, and speaks. Were a symbol needed of the Ireland that outbraved the terrors of centuries, and preserved her spiritual heritage despite the ravages of bitterest persecution, it would be found in that grand old woman. There, in the middle of the road, within sound of the sea and in sight of the altar, we see her, by the might of spiritual force conquering even death itself. With hands outstretched and face uplifted, she looks at the priest saying the august Mass, till, her glorious act of homage accomplished, she utters her last cry of dying life and deathless faith in the twin-loves of her indefectible soul: "Eternal praise to the Blessed Virgin's Son."

---

[66] *Sermons and Lectures* (New York, 1904), pp. 603–4.

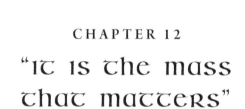

CHAPTER 12

"It is the mass that matters"

THE SUPERNATURAL LIFE OF the Irish people is not a writer's fancy or a poet's dream. It is a great spiritual fact. Fifteen hundred years ago, the nation was born into Christ, the grace of God flooded her soul, the beauty of the Faith captivated her heart, and she has clung to it ever since. Notwithstanding all the persistent attempts to rob her, she has resolutely refused to give it up. She has passed it on from generation to generation. Her children are daily, one by one, incorporated into "the Blessed Virgin's Son," and the supernatural life poured into them in Baptism, augmented in Confirmation, and sublimated in Communion elevates their natural life and colors their national existence.

Reduced to two-thirds of the population by the middle of the eighteenth century, they again mounted up, and toward the middle of the nineteenth, were in a majority of six to one. In spite of the consequences of the famine of 1847, in spite of wholesale evictions of tenants, heartrending dispersion of families, and other causes of depopulation, the Catholics of Ireland have always rejoiced in a prolific blessing, and are now in a majority of three to one.

A systematic attempt had been made to destroy the race, but the race lived on. Even when the enemy seemed to have triumphed, the Catholic Church showed no signs of dying. "Beauty's ensign was still crimson on her lips and on her cheeks, and death's pale flag was not advanced there."

The pale flag began, instead, to advance in the Church that was established in Ireland in the reign of Elizabeth for the express purpose of "converting" the Irish Catholics and that had been the instrument of as vile a persecution as ever disgraced the annals of religion. Already condemned, even by those who would have been glad of its success, it was once more, in the second half of the nineteenth century, weighed in the balance and finally found wanting. That it had failed egregiously to effectuate the intention for which it was originally planted was proved beyond doubt in the English House of Commons, and despite the most determined opposition, it was disestablished in the year 1869.

Since then it has been gradually declining in influence. Its press is now quite silent in places where once it was loudly vocal, many of its churches have been converted to purely secular uses, several of them, up and down the country, have been closed, and grass is growing on the paths that were once trodden by the feet of the few that went to weekly service.

The Catholic Church, on the contrary, has been all this time renewing its youth, showing daily increasing signs of life, clothing itself with fresh beauty, and revealing a glory that was never equaled even in the brightest days of the past. Convents and chapels stud the land, churches and schools are in every town and village, glorious temples, enshrining our eucharistic God and rejoicing in the Daily Sacrifice, proudly lift their spires to Heaven, emblematic of Irish history and symbolic of Catholic Faith.

Had England remained Catholic, not only would the Reformation never have come but "the whole Protestant movement would have collapsed before a hundred years were passed. The English State — and the English State alone — saved Protestantism."[67] And

---

[67]   Hollis, *The Monstrous Regiment*, p. 26.

yet, even in the very country that saved it, in the country on which it was originally imposed by force, as in every other place, it has proved a failure. Not only that, but it is one of the revenges of time that the main object of its venomous attack, the Mass, is today becoming, more and more, the center of careful attention, the chief matter of reverent examination, and a decisive factor in its disintegration.

Nearly half a century ago, this was foretold by a prominent English litterateur, who disturbed the intellectuals of his country by a striking article in an important magazine. While persons in high places were speaking and writing about "the growing power of Popery," and trying to persuade the common people that the great cataclysm of the sixteenth century in England was only a mere "rupture with Rome" and not "a re-settlement of religion on a new footing," Mr. Augustine Birrell[68] gave expression to some plain truths and more than one prophecy.

"Our children," he wrote, "if not our august selves, will make up their minds what happened at the Reformation, and my suggestion is that they will do so in a majority of cases ... by concentrating their attention upon what will seem to them most important. And especially will they bend their minds upon the Mass."

"Nobody nowadays," he continues, "save a handful of vulgar fanatics, speaks irreverently of the Mass. If the Incarnation be indeed the one divine event to which the whole creation moves, the miracle of the altar may well seem its restful shadow cast over a dry and thirsty land for the help of man, who is apt to be discouraged if perpetually told that everything really important and interesting happened once for all, long ago, in the chill historic past."

Discouragement for this reason can, however, never touch the Catholic, for he knows well that at least one very interesting thing, one really important thing that happened once, long ago, the great

---

[68] Birrell, *The Nineteenth Century* (April 1896).

Oblation on Calvary, happens again, in an unbloody manner, every day and every hour, aye and every minute, in some part of the world, from the rising to the setting of the sun. It happens as often as a Catholic priest stands at the altar; for, not only is the Eucharist the memory of a sacrifice, but it is "a real and proper sacrifice." It is a sacrifice complete, intended by Christ Himself, in His unfathomable love, not only to recall but to re-present, to "show forth the death of Christ till He come," and to apply to our souls the superabundant fruits of the Sacrifice of the Cross.

"All Masses are one sacrifice," says Adrian Fortescue,[69] "including the death of the Cross, continuing through all time the act of offering then begun. So at every Mass, in a real sense, we kneel at the foot of the Cross. The centuries that have passed since the first Good Friday are nothing before God. With God there is no time; a thousand years before His eyes are as yesterday that passed. Every time we hear Mass we look across that gulf of time, we are again before the Cross, with His Mother and St. John; we offer still that Victim then slain, present here under the form of bread and wine. The act of Calvary is an integral part of every Mass. It is of the altar of Calvary that we eat when we make our Communion."

Every Catholic feels this in the inmost shrine of his heart, and to him, therefore, "the miracle of the altar," the Sacrifice of the Mass, is indeed a "restful shadow" under which all who believe may take shelter from "the heat and the burden of the day." It is a "bright cloud" from which light and peace, love and loyalty, courage and heroism stream down, to the music of the solemn words of God the Father: "This is my beloved Son, in whom I am well pleased: hear ye him" (Matt. 17:5).

In the Mass, He adores, thanks, supplicates, and satisfies on our behalf. He pays to His heavenly Father the four great debts we owe

---

[69] *The Roman Missal*, p. vi.

Him as sinful rational creatures. Those who communicate at Mass participate most fully in His august action, get into closest touch with Him, feel the sweetness of His kiss, and have the "dry and thirsty land" of their hearts bedewed with grace that will bring forth abundant fruit.

Perhaps the non-Catholic writer already quoted understood most of this as every Catholic understands it all, for he links Communion and the Mass together in sentences that cannot easily be forgotten. After having said that "it is doubtful whether any poor sinful child of Adam (not being a paid agent of the Protestant Alliance) ever witnessed, even ignorantly … the Communion Service according to the Roman Catholic ritual without emotion," he *immediately* adds one of the deepest appreciations as well as one of the most arresting prophecies regarding the Mass.

"It is," he writes, "the Mass that matters; it is the Mass that makes the difference; so hard to define, so subtle it is, yet so perceptible, between a Catholic country and a Protestant one, between Dublin and Edinburgh, between Havre and Cromer.

"Here, I believe, is one of the battle-fields of the future."

The difference thus referred to is due to the radiated influence of the Eucharist, to the virtue that goes out from the Mass, creating an *atmosphere* that is subtle indeed, and yet quite perceptible, especially to one who has the Faith. Such a one feels it easily in Catholic cities such as Havre and Dublin, but never in Protestant ones. Mass and Communion unite us indeed with Christ our Head, but also through Him with all His members. "For we, being many, are one bread, one body: all that partake of one bread" (1 Cor. 10:17). This one heavenly Bread binds us all together in such a way that our supernatural unity in Christ becomes a grand accomplished fact. The Eucharist is the Sacrament of union, of peace, and of love.

And as Communion is never merely an individual act, so neither is Mass.

> The Mass is always essentially a community act; and this
> is not merely in the sense that the whole community
> should take part in it, but also and emphatically in the
> sense that participation in the one Bread gives the com-
> munity its true cohesion and unity, and builds it up into
> the supernatural organism of the Body of Christ, in which
> form it is presented to the Father by the hand of the divine
> High Priest.... The Eucharist is not the Sacrament of the
> personal Christ alone; it is also at the same time ... the
> Sacrament of the mystical Christ. It is a community thing
> through and through.[70]

However much this may be overlooked at the present time, to the great
detriment of peace and love, it must have been realized by our brave
forefathers when they gathered together in the deep glen, the mountain
shieling, or the damp cave to assist at the Holy Sacrifice of the Mass.
They surely were then imbued with the thought that, though few, they
were yet many; not mere isolated worshippers, but members of one
great Body, being in communion with the whole Church of Christ. They
knew that though cut off by cruel laws and watchful soldiers, by wary
spies and bloodthirsty priest-catchers, they were yet bound together by
the Bread of Life that came from the altar of God.

The eucharistic spirit poured into their souls was a spirit of
burning charity and splendid sacrifice, which united them, not
merely shoulder to shoulder, but heart to heart in magnificent soli-
darity in Christ. In this spirit, they stood up in proud and unconquerable defiance against the great enemy of their religion and the very
gates of Hell. In this spirit, and with the grand consciousness of all it
meant, they fought the good fight and finished their course. They
finished their course in poverty and suffering, in the dungeon or on
the scaffold, but they kept the Faith in order that they might hand on

---

[70] Karl Adam, *Christ our Brother*, p. 74.

to us, and that we might hand on to our children, undimmed and unimpaired, the bright torch of that same Faith and the precious heirloom of the august Mass.

We honor these as our greatest heroes, though they are despised by "the wise and prudent" of this enlightened age. They were ignorant, if you will, because they were cruelly deprived of the benefits of education. They were poor, it is true, because they were brutally robbed of the goods of this world. But though deprived of the benefits of education, their minds were aglow with supernatural light, and though robbed of the goods of earth, they were dowered with the gifts of Heaven. They had hope that God would one day remove the dark cloud that hung, like a pall of death, over their dear and desolate land. They had faith that, though driven from their cathedrals and churches and mud hovels, He would be with them still in the mountains and the bogs and the caves till better days should dawn. They had love, too, that Christ Himself inspired and that made them cling in an agony of hopeless affection to their ruined altars and desecrated shrines, even as Mary Magdalene clung to the empty sepulcher where the Body of Jesus had been laid.

They sorrowed as she sorrowed, they yearned as she yearned, and they, too, said to the angels that still were guarding those holy places: "They have taken away my Lord: and I know not where they have laid him" (John 20:13). No! They knew not where He was laid and were wandering about the mountains and hills until the sound of a horn or the blast of a bugle told them that He was already nigh. Then, as the heart of the Irish exile beats faster when he catches a glimpse of the fair hills of his native land, as the soul of the true friend grows warmer when he clasps once more the hand of his home-returned friend, even as the stag panteth for the fountains of living water, so did the hearts of these men and women beat faster, and grow warmer, and pant for one short glance of the God of their hearts' devotion.

And wherever the poor hunted Irish priest selected his temporary altar, *there* were keen Irish eyes ever ready to look out on the hilltops for the human bloodhounds on his track. *There* were faithful Irish hands ever willing to hold the two brown candles lest they should be quenched by wind or rain. And *there* also were warm Irish Catholic people in whose souls burned a passion of devotion, on whose lips thrilled the language of prayer, as they looked upward at the mystic moment of the elevation: "Mo ghrádh, Thu, a Iosa! Céad mile fáilte romhat, a Thighearna! Céad mile fáilte romhat, a ghrádh ghil mo chroidhe 'stigh!" *You* are my love, O Jesus! A hundred thousand welcomes before You, O Lord! A hundred thousand welcomes before You, O bright (white) love of my heart within!

"STILL THEIR SPIRIT
WALKS ABROAD"

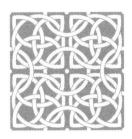

LET US PAUSE HERE for a while and look back before we hasten forward to a close. We are too ignorant of our past. Of our profane history some of us know but little, and of our sacred history even less. Yet, from the one might be learned many an incident to make us love more fervently our native land, and from the other many a lesson to make us more loyal to the Church, the priest, and the Mass.

Our sacred history tells us of a time when no altar or church was allowed, and even when the latter was at length permitted, there dared not be the simplest steeple to beautify it, nor the smallest bell to call the faithful to divine worship. It recalls a period when the priest was hunted like a wild beast, and when the same price was put upon his head as upon that of a wolf. It speaks of an age when the Mass was proscribed as an idolatrous rite and when its celebration, or even assistance at it, was punished by imprisonment or banishment, confiscation or death.

But the Irish people met all this with unshaken resolution, and not all the many devices of devilish ingenuity could tear from their hearts the love of the Mass, nor the craving to assist at it. To reach the appointed place in time for Mass, even men and women advanced in years often set out the previous night and traveled long distances in frost and snow to lay the homage of their souls' fidelity before their eucharistic Lord in the cold grey dawn of the morning.[71]

They sheltered the priest in spite of every penalty and never betrayed him for the most tempting reward. They clung tenaciously to their religion. They fought valiantly for the Mass, and though they fell, they did not fail.

> They never fail who die
> In a great cause. The block may soak their gore;
> Their heads may sodden in the sun; their limbs
> Be strung to city gates, and castle walls —
> But still their spirit walks abroad.

It walked abroad especially during eucharistic week, and as I sat in the Phoenix Park waiting for the High Mass that crowned that imperishable time, I felt almost as if my own spirit were one with theirs. Back went my mind to 1679, when St. Oliver Plunkett, archbishop of Armagh, and Dr. Peter Talbot, archbishop of Dublin, lay side by side in the darkened cells of Dublin Castle. Back it went ten years more when there were but few priests and only one bishop, Dr. Patrick Plunket of Ardagh, in residence in Ireland; and still much farther back to 1584, when another brave archbishop, Dr. Dermot O'Hurley of Cashel, was hanged with the gad on a quiet June morning at Gallows Green.

But my mind rested most on the little procession that marched through the city of Dublin just exactly three centuries ago. And when the raucous cry of the heretics struck the ears of my spirit: "Och, Ochón! The Pope is dead. The Mass is gone," it was answered quickly by the cheering prophecy of the Capuchin: "But the truth, I hope, shall prove contrary with an Alleluia, singing: The Pope is alive, and the Mass is come home."

---

[71] Moran, *Spicilegium Ossoriense*, vol. 2 , p. 472.

The truth had indeed proved very contrary, and on that unforgettable Sunday, as I looked in subdued delight on the vast hosting of over a million Catholic men and women, my heart murmured again and again a fervent *Deo Gratias* that the gloom of the past was gone and that the glory of the present was ours. The prophecy of the humble but hopeful Capuchin had at last been fulfilled in a manner resplendent beyond his wildest hopes and dreams. After the lapse of three hundred years of checkered history, the Alleluia, singing, "The Pope is alive, and the Mass is come home," was making music in every heart. Not only was it making music in thousands upon thousands of Irish hearts, but it was now being translated into hymns of jubilant praise to God Who had preserved the Faith in Irish souls and made it at last shine forth before the enraptured eyes of the whole world with a pomp and pageantry that had never before been seen on earth.

The pope, far from being dead, was in our very midst, full of life and dignity and fatherly love, in the person of a cardinal legate, whom the people had already taken completely to their hearts. Yea, at the conclusion of the Pontifical High Mass, the Holy Father's own warm soul got into closest union with ours, and in a phrase that touched the springs of feeling and thrilled many a worshipper, we heard his living, loving voice say, "We are with you as a Father is with his son, rejoicing to share ... directly and in person, your joy and the triumph of the Eucharist."

That indeed was the meaning of the unsurpassably glorious week for the whole world, *but it was still more its special and radiant meaning for Ireland.* The winter of humiliation was past. The rain of persecution was over and gone. The flowers of religious devotion were blooming at their fullest in our land, and here, in very truth, was the unparalleled triumph of the Eucharist in the capital of our country, which was once red with the blood of martyrs, and in the hearts of a people who are the descendants of "recusants" and of saints.

The triumph was writ large over the whole week. It was writ in the streets and the lanes; it was writ on the foldings of the sky; it was writ at the gateway of the stars; it was writ, above all, on the altars of the churches and chapels of our land. The proscribed Mass had "come home" to every city and town and parish, and deluged the Metropolis with tide after tide of grace that is flowing still. More Masses were said in Dublin during that week than, perhaps, were ever said before in any part of the world within the same time, and love of the great Sacrifice of our Faith increased to the intensity of a strong white light that, we pray God, may continue to endure.

It is certain to endure if only we remember the past of which the present is the fruit and translate its heroic memories into living actualities. That we should ever remember it is the earnest wish of the Vicar of Christ himself who gave a special commission to his legate, Cardinal Lorenzo Lauri, as he was about to start for Ireland. Having commanded him to tell the Irish people of the great happiness he felt because of their wonderful devotion to the Blessed Sacrament, the Holy Father added, in a letter that was read in the Pro-Cathedral, Dublin, at the opening of the eucharistic congress: "Exhort them to be faithful followers of the example of their forefathers.... Arouse their spirits so that, never forgetful of the 'Mass-Rock,' they shall faithfully cherish devotion to the Holy Eucharist as the standard of their Faith, and as a defence against errors."

Their spirits were indeed aroused by the addresses of the cardinal legate, but they were particularly stirred on the memorable Thursday night when, in the Phoenix Park, the voice of His Grace, Most Rev. Dr. Glennon, archbishop of St. Louis, USA, rang out over the heads of a quarter of a million of Irish Catholics. In burning words that came from the depths of his soul, he recalled the time when "the pastor was stricken, and the flock dispersed," when there was "a torch for the chapel, a noose for the priest, and a sword for the people."

The standard of the Eucharist was raised even more triumphantly than ever in the history of our country on that unforgettable occasion and was committed to the care of the 250,000 men who represented the entire resurgent nation. That they might hold it proudly aloft and never allow it to fall from their grasp, that they might pass it on to their children, the eloquent preacher, speaking in the presence of the apostolic legate, and of the princes, prelates, priests, and people from many lands, flung out his voice in triumph and told the kindly visitors from the continent that Ireland's Catholicity consisted in something "more than her memories and her ruins." "Italy," he said, as the vast crowd looked with riveted gaze and listened in tense silence, "Italy may have her glorious basilicas, France her stately cathedrals, England her regrets, but Ireland has her holy places, her martyrs, and her 'Mass-Rocks.' But more than that, in the hearts of her people dwells a faith as adamantine as the granite walls that guard their island shore."

The men and women who died for the Faith, the worshippers that clustered round the "Mass-Rocks" are gone indeed. *"But still their spirit walks abroad."* It walks abroad in this land of ours in which religious and national ideals have ever been blended, in which Faith and Fatherland, and not Fatherland and Faith, was always, is still, and, please God, ever will be the glorious rallying cry.

And through this spirit, we are made conscious of the vibrant appeal that comes to us across centuries of oppression from the strong hearts of millions of dauntless men and women of our race. They call to us to remember the price they paid even in their hearts' blood, and invigorated by this remembrance, to guard our Catholic Faith, to cleave to the pope and the Mass, to continue to hold aloft the standard of the Eucharist, and to be as devoted to it, as Sacrament and Sacrifice in these bright and peaceful days as they were in dark and troubled times.

They exhort us to be generous, to rise in the morning as they often rose at night, and to repair to the church where the august Mass is to be said. They beseech us to approach the altar regularly, nay frequently, and to strengthen our piety with a knowledge of the real meaning as well as the *social* signification of the great Sacrifice and the intimate Communion. Then, too, in proper liturgical order, they urge at least an occasional visit of affectionate gratitude to the tabernacle where Jesus still waits in love.

There, where "the Catholic soul enacts its most sacred hours," *there*, where "it drinks in life in its deepest, most divine quintessence," *there*, where "all time is silent and eternity speaks," *there*, within sight of the sanctuary lamp, and in the light of the face of Him we love, the truth will blaze upon us of Ireland's loyalty to the Mass.

In that holy quiet, in that hushed place, the spirits of our forefathers will speak to us as in no other spot on earth. In that sanctified silence, in that solemn stillness, they must surely be heard, for their whisper will sound in our ears like the voice of many waters, as, pointing to the Shrine of deathless Love, they say, "Jesus is *there* now surrounded with flowers and encircled with light. But time was when there were no flowers, save those of devotion that bloomed in bleeding Irish hearts, and when there was no light, save that of Faith which burned brightly in generous Irish souls. Those spiritual flowers must continue to bloom; that supernatural light must continue to glow; and may both be fostered and fed by 'Piety's own Celtic tongue' in which we breathed forth our warmest and latest prayers."

O spirits of the martyrs of faithful Ireland! O spirits of the lovers of the beautiful Mass! We are touched by your prayer and will answer your appeal. Impress your Catholic Faith deep on our hearts. Put your Irish language again sweet upon our lips. Make us even more Catholic and more Irish so that we may cling with ever-increasing loyalty to the sublime Sacrifice of the Altar for which you suffered so terribly, and yet so gladly, because you loved it with a love that was deep as the sea, ardent as fire, and stronger than death.

bibliography

A Tour through Ireland, by Two Gentlemen. Dublin: 1748.

Analecta Hibernica, No. 4. Dublin: 1932.

Angelus. Pages from the Story of the Irish Capuchins. Cork: 1915.

———. "Dusty Documents." The Capuchin Annual. 1931.

———. "More Dusty Documents." The Capuchin Annual. 1932.

Archbold, Nicholas. Evangellical Fruict of the Seraphicall
Franciscan Order. MS. Dublin: 1630.

———. Historie of the Irish Capucins. MS. Dublin: 1643.

Belloc, Hilaire. How the Reformation Happened. London: 1928.

———. James the Second. London: 1928.

———. Cranmer. London: 1931.

Birrell, Augustine. The Nineteenth Century. 1896.

Burke, William P. Irish Priests in Penal Times. Waterford: 1914.

Carrigan, William. History and Antiquities of the Diocese of
Ossory. 4 vols. Dublin: 1905.

Cogan, A. Diocese of Meath, Ancient and Modern. 3 vols. Dublin: 1862–70.

Comerford, M. Collections Relating to the Diocese of Kildare and Leighlin. 3 vols. Dublin: 1883–86.

Concannon, Mrs. Thomas. The Blessed Eucharist in Irish History. Dublin: 1932.

D'Alton, E. A. History of Ireland. Vol. 2, From 1547 to 1782.

de Blácam, Aodh. Gaelic Literature Surveyed. Dublin: 1929.

Egan, P. M. History, Guide and Directory of County and City of Waterford. Kilkenny: n.d.

Fitzpatrick, William John. Life, Times, and Correspondence of the Right Rev. Dr. Doyle. 2 vols. Dublin: 1861.

Fletcher, J. S. The Reformation in Northern England. London: 1925.

Gasquet, Francis Aidan. Henry the Eighth and the English Monasteries. Pop. ed. London: 1899.

Henley, P. Spenser in Ireland. Cork: 1928.

Hollis, Christopher. The Monstrous Regiment. London: 1929.

Hynes, Michael J. The Mission of Rinuccini. Dublin: 1932.

Irish Historical Documents. No. 3. A Bishop of the Penal Times. Cork: 1933.

Joyce, P. W. Irish Names of Places. 2 vols. 7th ed. Dublin: 1901.

Macaulay, Thomas Babington. Miscellaneous Writings and Speeches. Pop. ed.

Maguire, E. History of the Diocese of Raphoe. 2 vols. Dublin: n.d.

Meehan, C. P. Rise and Fall of the Franciscan Monasteries. 2nd ed. Dublin: 1869.

——. Fate and Fortunes of O'Neill and O'Donnell. 2nd ed. Dublin: 1886.

Mitchel, John. Reply to the Falsification of History by James Anthony Froude, entitled "The English in Ireland." Glasgow and London, n.d.

Moran, Patrick. History of the Catholic Archbishops of Dublin. Vol. 1. Dublin: 1864.

——. Life of the Most Rev. Oliver Plunket. Dublin: 1870.

——. Spicilegium Ossoriense. 3 vols. Dublin: 1874, 1876, 1884.

——. Persecution of Irish Catholics under Cromwell. Dublin: 1884.

——, ed. Rothe's Analecta. Dublin: 1884.

——. Catholics in Ireland under the Penal Laws in the Eighteenth Century. London: 1899.

Murphy, Denis S. J. Our Martyrs. Dublin: 1896.

——. Cromwell in Ireland. Dublin: 1902.

O'Cianáin, Tadhg. Flight of the Earls. Edited by Paul Walsh. Dublin: 1916.

O'Clery. Life of Red Hugh O'Donnell. Edited by Denis Murphy. Dublin: 1895.

O'Rourke. The Battle of the Faith in Ireland. Dublin: 1887.

O'Sullivan, Philip. Historiae Catholicae Iberniae Compendium. Edited by M. Kelly. Dublin: 1850.

Pastor, Ludwig. The History of the Popes. Vol. 8.

————. The History of the Popes. Vol. 13.

Power, Irish Historical Documents.

Prendergast, John. Cromwellian Settlement. Dublin: 1865.

Ronan, Myles V. Reformation in Dublin. London: 1926.

————. Reformation in Ireland under Elizabeth. London: 1930.

Sheed, F. J., ed. The Irish Way. London: 1932.

Shirley, Evelyn Philip. Original Letters and Papers in Illustration of the History of the Church in Ireland. London: 1851.

Stanislaus. "The Rinuccini Memoirs." The Capuchin Annual. 1932.

Travels of Sir William Brereton in Ireland. Edited by Litton Falkiner. In Illustrations of Irish History. London: 1904.

about the author

Fr. Augustine Hayden, O.F.M. Cap. (1870–1954), Capuchin priest, nationalist, and Irish language advocate, was celebrated for his talents as a missionary and lecturer, and he delivered retreats across Ireland. He was a prolific writer and penned a number of devotional texts, including *St. Francis and the Blessed Eucharist* and *Ireland's Loyalty to Mary*. Fr. Hayden tirelessly served the faithful even amid violence and turmoil.